The Philosophy of Ted Chiang

David Friedell
Editor

The Philosophy of Ted Chiang

Editor
David Friedell
Philosophy
Union College
Schenectady, NY, USA

ISBN 978-3-031-81661-1   ISBN 978-3-031-81662-8   (eBook)
https://doi.org/10.1007/978-3-031-81662-8

© The Editor(s) (if applicable) and The Author(s), under exclusive license to Springer Nature Switzerland AG 2025

This work is subject to copyright. All rights are solely and exclusively licensed by the Publisher, whether the whole or part of the material is concerned, specifically the rights of translation, reprinting, reuse of illustrations, recitation, broadcasting, reproduction on microfilms or in any other physical way, and transmission or information storage and retrieval, electronic adaptation, computer software, or by similar or dissimilar methodology now known or hereafter developed.
The use of general descriptive names, registered names, trademarks, service marks, etc. in this publication does not imply, even in the absence of a specific statement, that such names are exempt from the relevant protective laws and regulations and therefore free for general use.
The publisher, the authors and the editors are safe to assume that the advice and information in this book are believed to be true and accurate at the date of publication. Neither the publisher nor the authors or the editors give a warranty, expressed or implied, with respect to the material contained herein or for any errors or omissions that may have been made. The publisher remains neutral with regard to jurisdictional claims in published maps and institutional affiliations.

Cover illustration: © Don Landwehrle / Alamy

This Palgrave Macmillan imprint is published by the registered company Springer Nature Switzerland AG.
The registered company address is: Gewerbestrasse 11, 6330 Cham, Switzerland

If disposing of this product, please recycle the paper.

For Kaia

Foreword

In his *Republic*, Plato has Socrates describe a curious scenario to his student Glaucon:

> Imagine human beings living in an underground den which is open towards the light; they have been there from childhood, having their necks and legs chained, and can only see into the den. At a distance there is a fire, and between the fire and the prisoners a raised way, and a low wall is built along the way, like the screen over which marionette players show their puppets. Behind the wall appear moving figures, who hold in their hands various works of art, and among them images of men and animals, wood and stone, and some of the passers-by are talking and others silent.

This is, of course, the Allegory of the Cave, and Plato offers it as a way of explaining his theory of Forms.

Elsewhere in his writings Plato explains the theory of Forms in more straightforward terms—for example, when he says that beautiful things are beautiful because they partake of Beauty itself—and if we're going to judge that theory, we must do so on the strength of those arguments. So why did Plato offer the allegory of the Cave? Because the image of people watching shadows on a wall is clear and evocative, it engages the attention of non-philosophers in a way that Plato's other explanations do not. And that's something science fiction can do too: it recasts abstract arguments into a more concrete and relatable form. Plato wasn't writing science fiction, but his allegory of the Cave demonstrates the usefulness of storytelling when trying to explain a philosophical idea.

I like philosophy, but a lot of philosophical questions are debated in highly theoretical terms, making it easy for non-philosophers to wonder why anyone should care about the answer. One of the strengths of science fiction is its ability to illustrate why someone might care. In the here and now, a philosophical question might be strictly theoretical, but in the world of a science fiction story, it could have practical consequences. That means there could be inhabitants of that world for whom the answer to that question is hugely important. If a writer can make a sympathetic protagonist out of one of those inhabitants, the readers will appreciate the significance of that question on a visceral, emotional level rather than a purely intellectual one.

Having said that, I should note that I don't start writing with the intention of dramatizing a philosophical question. As an example, let me talk about the inspiration for my story "Anxiety is the Dizziness of Freedom." It's a story about the implications of the many-worlds interpretation on free will, but I never thought, "I want to write about MWI and free will." Instead, the story originated with some idle thoughts about the way science fiction typically depicts travel between parallel universes. To be specific: whenever a character uses their wrist-mounted device to hop into another universe, how are they specifying their destination? If you assigned each parallel universe a number, simply entering the number of the universe you wanted would take the rest of your life.

Suppose all you're trying to do is communicate with someone in a parallel universe. Then you avoid the problem of how matter actually gets moved from one universe to the other, but the issue of how the transmitter and the receiver establish a connection is another version of the same question: how do you precisely specify the universe you're interested in? (As a side note: why do we so readily accept that travel between universes could be done using a single device, but communicating between universes requires two devices? The former involves transmitting matters, while the latter only involves transmitting information. I suspect the answer has to do with our relationship to storytelling conventions.) Then it occurred to me that this problem could be solved if you posited that the transmitter and the receiver *were originally the same device*; the activation of the device marks the branch point between the two universes. The problem of how you specify the universe you want goes away, because there's a unique device for each pair of universes, and you can only contact the other universe that resulted from the activation of a particular device.

It was then that I started thinking about what kind of story I could tell with such devices. Unlike the "go anywhere in the multiverse" potential of typical parallel-universe stories, the scenarios opened up by these devices were far more restricted in scope. It seemed to me that people would be interested in learning the consequences of their individual choices, which is when I realized I would be writing about free will (again).

As I was thinking about what situations might be dramatically interesting, I wound up rereading Daniel Dennett's *Freedom Evolves*, which argues for compatibilist free will, as well as getting a copy of Robert Kane's *The Significance of Free Will*, which argues for libertarian free will. I like Kane's book, but I find Dennett more persuasive. I believe in physicalism and compatibilism, and I knew I wanted my story to reflect those beliefs, but I hadn't really thought a lot about how the many-worlds interpretation affect free will, so I had to figure out my position on that. I don't believe that quantum indeterminacy plays a role in human decision making, so I don't see how a person making different choices would give rise to different universes; I came to the conclusion that branching has to precede a person choosing different options rather than resulting from it.

In the process of writing the story, I clarified my own thinking about certain philosophical questions, but I can't say that was my original goal. Neither can I say it was just a byproduct; I needed clarity in order to tell a story that I could be satisfied with. Is this anything like what philosophers go through when they write their papers? I don't know. There's a piece of writing advice I like, which is that it's important to figure out what your story is saying and then decide whether you're okay with that message; if you want to publish a story with a message you disagree with, at least do it deliberately. I suspect most philosophers sincerely believe in the arguments they make in their papers, although I can't be sure.

And of course, fiction assumes a willing suspension of disbelief on the part of the reader that philosophy papers do not. I enjoy a certain degree of philosophical sophistication when I read science fiction, but I don't expect it to meet the standards of actual philosophers. This is similar to my feeling about scientific accuracy; I derive a special pleasure from science fiction that contains real science, but it'd be unreasonable to expect science fiction to adhere to science completely. First and foremost, science fiction needs to be good art, and a certain amount of real science or real philosophy can help with that, but if pursuing absolute accuracy would interfere with the author's artistic goals, art should take priority.

It is both gratifying and flattering to learn that despite whatever poetic license I've taken and suspension of disbelief I've relied on, philosophers have found my work engaging enough to write about. I will never be a philosopher, but if my speculations don't make philosophers roll their eyes, I count that as a success.

Seattle, WA, USA   Ted Chiang

Acknowledgments

I want to extend my utmost gratitude to everyone who participated in a workshop on Ted Chiang and Philosophy that I organized at Union College in the Spring of 2022: Mark Balaguer, Kiki Berk, Rebecca Chan, Ted Chiang, Noelle Leslie Dela Cruz, Don Fallis, Hannah Kim, Harper Lyon, Ned Markosian, Rhys Moger, Bradley Rettler, and Katherine Ward. Their participation and the conversations we had did much to strengthen this project and move it forward. I would like to thank Union College, Union College's Philosophy Department, and the Ichabod Spencer Foundation for their generous support of that workshop. Many thanks to Leahanna Pelish and Krisanna Scheiter for all of their help with organizing the workshop.

I am very grateful to all of the authors who contributed to this volume, and also to Robin James and Amy Invernizzi at Palgrave Macmillan for their enthusiasm and support for this project. Thanks also to Elizabeth Scarbrough for their excellent work on the index.

A big thank you to Ted Chiang for writing the Foreword. Whoever said not to meet your heroes was wrong; it has been one of the great honors and pleasures of my career to meet with and work with Ted Chiang.

Last, but certainly not least, thanks to Kristina Flemming Friedell for her love and support.

Contents

Part I Free Will   1

1 Why the Market Value of Free Will is $99.99   3
   Mark Balaguer

2 Many-worlds and Free Will   11
   David Baker

Part II God   19

3 Death, God, and Meaning in Ted Chiang's Stories   21
   Kiki Berk

4 The Presence of Evil and the Absence of God   29
   Bradley Rettler

5 Mysterious Ways: Making Sense of God's Actions in
   Hell Is the Absence of God   37
   Gabriel Oak Rabin

Part III Technology   45

6   The Value of Fact and Feeling   47
Daniel Pallies

7   We Can Remember It for You Better: Ted Chiang on Technology and Human Knowledge   55
Don Fallis

Part IV Existentialism   65

8   How to Live With Freedom   67
Katherine Ward

9   Existential Responsibility in Kierkegaard, Nietzsche, and Chiang   75
Justin White

Part V Beauty   83

10   Just Looking: Check Out the Computational Topography on Her!   85
Lisa Bellantoni

11   Should You Like What You See? Ethics, Aesthetics, and the Appreciation of Human Beauty   95
Alyssa Izatt and Julia Minarik

Part VI Procreation Ethics   105

12   The Ethics of Making a Short Life   107
Audrey Benson and Mayah Teplitskiy

Part VII	Contradictions	115
13	Knowledge, Symbols, and Understanding Kenny Easwaran	117
14	Choosing What's Fictionally True Hannah H. Kim	127
Part VIII	Time	135
15	Time Machines and Predictors are Possible but Unlikely David Friedell	137
16	The Temporality of Our Emotions and Time in Ted Chiang's Stories Rebecca Chan	145
Part IX	Human and Alien Intelligence	153
17	Language, Thought, Experience, and Chiang's "Story of Your Life" Peter Murray	155
18	Jeopardy! and the Stories of Our Lives Benjamin Chan	165
19	What Is It to Understand Enlightenment? Johnathan Flowers	175

Part X Artificial Intelligence   185

20 Raising an AI Teenager   187
    Catherine Stinson

21 Save the Digients! On the Moral Status of AI   195
    Noelle Leslie Dela Cruz

Index   203

NOTES ON CONTRIBUTORS

David Baker is Professor of Philosophy at the University of Michigan. His research focuses on the philosophy of physics, metaphysics, and the philosophy of science. He has also published some short-form science fiction.

Mark Balaguer is Professor of Philosophy at California State University, Los Angeles. His research is primarily in metaphysics, free will, and the philosophy of mathematics. He is the author of five books: *Platonism and Anti-Platonism in Mathematics*; *Free Will as an Open Scientific Problem*; *Free Will*; *Metaphysics, Sophistry, and Illusion*; and *Mathematical Anti-Realism and Modal Nothingism*.

Lisa Bellantoni is Associate Professor of Philosophy at Albright College. Her research focuses on the ethical, social and political dimensions of emerging digital technologies.

Audrey Benson is a junior at Union College, specializing in Mathematics and Statistics.

Kiki Berk is Professor of Philosophy at Southern New Hampshire University. She received her Ph.D. in Philosophy from the VU University Amsterdam in 2010. Her current research interests are philosophy of death and philosophy of meaning in life.

Benjamin Chan is Assistant Professor of Philosophy at St. Norbert College. His research is primarily in ethics and trivia.

Rebecca Chan is Associate Professor of Philosophy at San José State University. She works primarily on metaphysics, philosophy of religion, and philosophy of law.

Noelle Leslie Dela Cruz is Full Professor of Philosophy at De La Salle University in Manila. She is author of the poetry collection *Sisyphus on the Penrose Stairs: Meta-Reveries* (Vagabond Press), lead author of *Philosophy of the Human Person: Giving Meaning to Life* (Oxford University Press), and co-editor of the anthology *Feminista: Gender, Race, and Class in the Philippines* (Anvil Press). Her research and teaching areas include existential phenomenology, philosophy of literature, and feminist philosophy.

Kenny Easwaran is a professor in the Department of Logic and Philosophy of Science at the University of California, Irvine. He works on issues regarding the role of probability and uncertainty in knowledge and decision-making, as well as the philosophy of mathematics.

Don Fallis is Professor of Philosophy and Computer Sciences at Northeastern University. He studies deception as well as the impact of technology on the acquisition of knowledge.

Johnathan Flowers is Assistant Professor of Philosophy at California State University, Northridge. His research is primarily in Japanese philosophy, American pragmatism, aesthetics, and philosophies of race, gender, disability, and sexuality.

David Friedell is Assistant Professor of Philosophy at Union College. His research is primarily in metaphysics, aesthetics, and the philosophy of language.

Alyssa Izatt is a PhD candidate in the Department of Philosophy at the University of British Columbia. Her research is supported by the Social Sciences and Humanities Research Council of Canada. She works primarily in moral philosophy and bioethics.

Hannah H. Kim is Assistant Professor of Philosophy at the University of Arizona. Her research is primarily in aesthetics, metaphysics, and Asian philosophy.

Julia Minarik is a PhD candidate at the University of Toronto. Her research is supported by the Social Sciences and Humanities Research

Council of Canada. Her current research on creativity lies at the intersection of aesthetics, epistemology, and the philosophy of mind.

Peter Murray is a teaching professor in the Philosophy Department at Skidmore College. His research is primarily in the philosophies of mind, language, action, and artificial intelligence.

Daniel Pallies is a research assistant professor at Lingnan University in Hong Kong. His research primarily concerns topics in moral psychology and the philosophy of well-being.

Gabriel Oak Rabin is Associate Professor of Philosophy at New York University Abu Dhabi and New York University. He has wide-ranging research interests in philosophy of mind, metaphysics, philosophy of language, and philosophy of mathematics. He has two cats and a lovely wife. He enjoys playing and composing music as well as adventuring in the great outdoors.

Bradley Rettler is Associate Professor of Philosophy at the University of Wyoming. He works on metaphysics, philosophy of religion, and bitcoin. He is a coauthor of both *Resistance Money: A Philosophical Case for Bitcoin* (Routledge Press) and *The Problem of Divine Personality* (Cambridge University Press).

Catherine Stinson is Queen's National Scholar in the Philosophical Implications of Artificial Intelligence, and Assistant Professor of Philosophy and Computing at Queen's University. Their research is primarily in philosophy of AI, philosophy of psychiatry, and ethical AI.

Mayah Teplitskiy is a senior at Union College, specializing in Mathematics and Philosophy. She will be starting a PhD in Mathematics at Boston College.

Katherine Ward is Assistant Professor of Philosophy at Bucknell University. She researches phenomenology and epistemology, and her recent book, *Standpoint Phenomenology*, explores phenomenological methodology through the lens of feminist standpoint epistemology.

Justin White is Associate Professor of Philosophy at Brigham Young University. His research focuses on nineteenth- and twentieth-century European philosophy, philosophy of agency, and moral psychology.

PART I

Free Will

CHAPTER 1

Why the Market Value of Free Will is $99.99

Mark Balaguer

1.1 Introduction

In Ted Chiang's story "What's Expected of Us," a machine is invented that predicts with 100% accuracy what people are about to do. When this happens, people become convinced that they don't have free will, and as a result, a third of the population descends into akinetic mutism—a kind of "walking coma." Maybe that would happen if we discovered that we don't have free will. But I'll argue in this chapter that if it did happen, it would involve a wild over-valuing of free will. Descending into akinetic mutism because you discovered that you didn't have free will would be like descending into akinetic mutism because you lost $100. Or so I'll argue.

M. Balaguer (✉)
Los Angeles, CA, USA
e-mail: mbalagu@calstatela.edu

1.2 Determinism

Let's start by asking how we could discover that we don't have free will. The most obvious answer to this question is that we could discover that *determinism* is true—i.e., that every event is *causally necessitated* by prior events together with the laws of nature.[1]

We can get a better understanding of determinism by thinking about pool balls. Imagine that you and I are playing pool and that I hit the cue ball and it goes into the corner pocket. It seems that, given the laws of nature, and given all the facts about the situation—how hard I hit the ball, how much spin I put on it, and so on—there was only *one* thing that the cue ball could have done. In other words, it seems that the way I hit the cue ball *determined* the path it would follow. It seems that the cue ball *couldn't have done anything else*. It seems that the laws of physics, together with all of the specific details about the situation, *forced* the cue ball to move in the exact way that it *did* move.

Determinism is the view that *all* events in the physical universe are like this. It's the view that every physical event is *completely causally necessitated* by prior events together with the laws of nature. Or to put the point differently, determinism is the view that every event has a cause that *makes* it happen exactly as it *does* happen.

If determinism is true, we get the following surprising result: as soon as the Big Bang occurred, it was already determined that the entire history of the universe would unfold exactly as it *has* unfolded. For instance, it was already determined 13 billion years ago that there would be a global pandemic in 2020. Why? Because if determinism is true, then every time something happens, there's only one next thing that can happen. So once the Big Bang happened, the next event was *forced on us* by the laws of physics; and then the next event after that was forced on us as well—and so on, all the way through history. So according to determinism, once the Big Bang occurred, it was an inevitable step-by-step 13-billion-year march to the 2020 pandemic.

And what goes for the 2020 pandemic goes for human decisions as well. Last night I went to an ice cream parlor, and there were 31 flavors to choose from, and I chose chocolate. It *seemed* that I chose of my own free

---

[1] The characters in Chiang's story discover not that determinism is true but that *eternalism* is true, which implies that the future already exists. But I think that eternalism is, perhaps surprisingly, compatible with full-blown free will, and so I think we should focus on determinism rather than eternalism.

will. But if determinism is true, then once the Big Bang occurred, it was already determined that I was going to choose chocolate. And that doesn't sound like free will. So it seems that if we discovered that determinism is true, then it would follow that we don't have free will.

1.3 Do-What-You-Want Free Will

There are actually *some* kinds of free will that are compatible with determinism. Consider, e.g., *do-what-you-want free will*, which is just the ability to choose and act in accordance with your desires—or, more simply, to do what you want. This sort of free will is compatible with determinism. To see why, notice that the following two claims could both be true:

> (i) Once the Big Bang occurred, it was already causally determined that 13 billion years later, I would have a *desire* to eat chocolate ice cream.
> (ii) My desire to eat chocolate ice cream caused me to order chocolate ice cream.

If these claims are both true, then my choice was causally determined by the Big Bang and the laws of nature. *But I still did what I wanted to do.* Indeed, my *want*—my *desire*—straightforwardly *caused* my choice. So, again, do-what-you-want free will is compatible with determinism.

But do-what-you-want free will is not the kind of free will that we could *discover* that we don't have. We know for certain that we do have this kind of free will because we've all had the experience of doing what we want. So if we're worried about discovering that we don't have free will, we're presumably thinking about a *different* kind of free will.

1.4 Not-Pre-Determined Free Will

Let's say that a person has *not-pre-determined free will* if and only if they make at least *some* decisions with the following two traits:

> (i) The decision was made *by the person in question* (in other words, the decision didn't just *happen* to the person; rather, the person *controlled* which option was chosen); and (ii) the decision wasn't causally determined by prior events.

So, for example, my decision to order chocolate ice cream was free in this not-pre-determined sense if (a) *I* made the decision, and (b) the decision wasn't *forced on me* by prior events—or, more succinctly, if (a) *I* did it, and (b) nothing *made* me do it.

Unlike do-what-you-want free will, not-pre-determined free will is incompatible with determinism. If our decisions are all causally determined by prior events, then we don't have not-pre-determined free will. So we could *discover* that we don't have not-pre-determined free will. And the question I want to ask is *how bad it would be*, if we discovered that we don't have not-pre-determined free will.

1.5 When Should We *Want* Free Will?

Let's start by asking *when*, during the course of our lives, we should want to have not-pre-determined free will. It might seem that we should want to have it whenever we're in a decision-making situation—whenever we need to choose one option from a set of possible options. But I don't think that's right; I think we should want to have not-pre-determined free will in only *some* decision-making situations. To bring this point out, let me start by defining two kinds of decisions:

> 1. *No-brainer decisions*: These are decisions in which it seems to you, in your conscious thinking, that your beliefs and desires and reasons-for-choosing pick out a *unique best option*, so that you're *certain* which option you want to choose.
>
> 2. *Torn decisions*: These are decisions in which (a) you feel completely torn between two or more live options—i.e., you have two or more tied-for-best options, and you have no conscious belief about which of them is best (they seem equally good to you)—and (b) you decide *while feeling torn* (because *just choosing* is better for some reason than remaining undecided).

Torn decisions are pretty rare. We usually go through life doing things without really thinking about it. For instance, if you're driving home from work and talking on the phone, you'll probably do all sorts of things without putting any thought into them at all—like putting your seat belt on, and starting your car, and turning into your driveway from your street. But this isn't what *all* of your actions are like. Every once in a while, you come to a "fork in the road," so to speak, and you stop and think about whether you want to pursue one course of action or another. And in some of these cases, you become completely torn about what to do and then you just *choose*—i.e., you make a *torn decision*.

I think we make torn decisions a few times a day. These decisions are usually pretty unimportant—they're usually about things like whether to order chocolate or vanilla ice cream, or whether to meet a friend for a drink or stay home and watch TV. But once in a while, we have to make torn decisions about important things. For example, you might have to choose between (a) accepting a great job offer that would require you to move to a city you hate and (b) passing on the job and remaining in the city you love. And you might have to decide while feeling completely torn—because you might have a deadline that forces you to choose while you still feel torn.

No-brainer decisions, on the other hand, are the exact opposite of this. These are decisions in which you feel completely certain which option is best. Suppose, for example, that I tell you that one minute from now, I'm going to give you either a million dollars or a poke in the eye with a sharp stick—and that you get to choose between these two options. If you're anything like me, this will be a no-brainer decision for you.

Now here's an observation: no one should want no-brainer decisions like this to be undetermined. We should all want the choosing of a million dollars to be straightforwardly caused by our reasons. Wanting this choice to be undetermined boils down to wanting there to be some chance—some non-zero probability—that you will choose the eye poking (or that an eye-poking choice will *occur in your head*, since it's hard to see how it could be the case that *you* make such a choice), *despite the fact that you don't* **want** *to choose the eye-poking option*. And no one should want that. What you should want, in cases like this, is for your choices to be caused by your reasons-for-choosing.

You might object here as follows: "We'll get a different result if we choose a less ridiculous case. Suppose, e.g., that Jane is trying to quit smoking but that she badly wants to smoke a cigarette right now. She has to decide whether to smoke a cigarette, and this seems like a no-brainer decision (because Jane's reasons-for-choosing pick out a unique best option—namely, not smoking). But surely we want not-pre-determined free will when we're in situations like this."

My response: This is *not* a no-brainer decision—because Jane has desires pulling her toward both options. Indeed, if Jane's current *felt* desire to smoke *feels exactly as strong to her* as her current felt desire to refrain from smoking, then this is a *torn* decision. A no-brainer decision is a decision in which your *whole self*—not just your "best self"—feels certain that one option is best. And my claim here is that no one should want decisions like *that* to be causally undetermined. (I'm sure that some people *do* want to have not-pre-determined free will in connection with no-brainer decisions, but they *shouldn't*—because it's not worthwhile.)

So when should we want not-pre-determined free will? Answer: when we're making *torn* decisions. Why? Because it's in torn-decisions that we find ourselves at a *crossroads*—having to choose between multiple possible paths that feel equally good to us. And so it's here that we want to be able to choose our *own* path, without anything *making* us choose one of the possible paths.[2]

1.6 What We'd Be Discovering, If We Discovered That We Don't Have Free Will

I just argued that we should want to have not-pre-determined free will in our torn decisions. But it's not clear that we *do*. Here are two possibilities:

> 1. *The Libertarian Scenario*: We do have not-pre-determined free will in at least some of our torn decisions. In other words, in at least some of your torn decisions, *you* control which option is chosen, and nothing *makes* you choose in the way that you do.
>
> 2. *The Deterministic Scenario*: We don't have not-pre-determined free will. More specifically, whenever you make a torn decision, there are always hidden prior events—events that occur before your choice and that you're unaware of—that completely cause you to choose a specific option. (We can assume that the hidden prior causes are nonconscious neural events that occur in your brain just before you choose, but other deterministic scenarios are possible, e.g., scenarios in which evil neuroscientists send signals into your brain that cause you to choose in specific ways.)

---

[2] I'm simplifying a bit. What I actually think is that (a) there's a continuum of possible decision types here (torn decisions and no-brainer decisions are at opposite ends of the spectrum, and in between, there are decisions in which you're *leaning toward* one option but aren't entirely certain that option is best); and (b) as we move down the spectrum from no-brainer decisions to torn decisions, our desire for not-pre-determined free will should increase, and it should max out in the limiting case of torn decisions. But we needn't worry about this complication here.

If what I've argued is correct, then (simplifying a bit) to discover that we don't have free will would be to discover that we're living in the deterministic scenario rather than the libertarian scenario. That, I think, would *suck*. I *hope* that we're living in the libertarian scenario. But how *badly* would it suck?

1.7 How Bad Would It Be?

One point to note here is that we're talking only about torn decisions, and again, we make torn decisions only a few times a day.[3] But the more important point, it seems to me, is that even if we're living in the deterministic scenario, it *feels* like we're living in the libertarian scenario. So even if we don't have not-pre-determined free will, we've got a *perfect forgery*. Suppose that your favorite painting is van Gogh's *Starry Night* and that you have a near-perfect copy of that painting in your house—so perfect that no human being could tell the difference between your forgery and the real painting. And now suppose that someone gave you the option to pay some money to switch your forgery for the real painting—but with the stipulation that you can't profit financially from the switch (e.g., suppose it was stipulated that you can't sell the painting or will it to anyone and that, upon your death, the two paintings will be switched back). How much would you be willing to pay to have the real *Starry Night* in your house, rather than the near-perfect forgery? Maybe *something*. But not *that* much, right? Maybe $100?

Living in the deterministic scenario would be just like having a perfect forgery of *Starry Night* in your house. Every time you made a torn decision, there would be some prior nonconscious neural event that caused you to choose a specific option. But the prior cause would be *hidden* from you. You wouldn't notice it at all. It would *feel* to you like *you* were doing the choosing—and that nothing was causing you to choose any specific option. We *know* that's how it would feel—because that's how it *does* feel when we make torn decisions. And if we discovered that determinism is true—and, hence, that we don't have not-pre-determined free will—nothing would change about how our torn decisions feel. And so in this

---

[3] You might want to add here that we make *important* torn decisions even more rarely. But I think the *little* decisions we make are just as important as the big ones—because we make so *many* of them. The courses of our lives are largely determined by the *mass* of little decisions that we make.

scenario, if we wished that we were living in the libertarian scenario, we'd be wishing for something that would feel *exactly* the same to us. We'd be wishing for something to be true, even though we wouldn't *notice* that it was true. How much would you be willing to pay for that? Would you be willing to give up a trip to Hawaii for something that you wouldn't even notice? I wouldn't. I'd pay *something*. But not a lot. I'm not an expert at pricing things, but I'd put the market value at about $99.99.

Perhaps you'll object that if we don't have not-pre-determined free will, then we're all victims of an illusion—and, hence, not living *authentic lives*. But we're victims of *many* illusions, and most of them don't undermine the authenticity of our lives. For instance, many of our ancestors believed that the sun goes around the earth, but this didn't make their lives less authentic. Now, you might respond that this illusion is unimportant—and that it's not linked to our sense of the kinds of beings we are. But if you think that, it's probably because you live in the twenty-first century. The belief that the earth is the center of the universe used to be extremely important to people. Indeed, the Catholic Church burned Bruno at the stake for, among other things, denying this claim.

I agree that *some* illusions would undermine the authenticity of our lives. If we were living in a Matrix-type scenario in which everything we experienced was part of a simulated fiction that was being fed into our brains by evil neuroscientists, then we wouldn't be living authentic lives. But I don't think the deterministic scenario—i.e., the scenario in which all of our torn decisions are causally determined by nonconscious neural events that occur just prior to choice—is analogous to the Matrix scenario. It seems more akin to the earth-isn't-the-center-of-the-universe scenario. Perhaps the deterministic scenario lies in between these other two scenarios—partway down the spectrum from the heliocentric scenario to the Matrix scenario. But I don't think it's very far down that path.

Chapter 2

Many-worlds and Free Will

David Baker

There is a real chance that we live in the sort of branching universe Ted Chiang portrays in "Anxiety is the Dizziness of Freedom." I've studied this question for a couple of decades, arguing back and forth with some of the world's experts on the subject. Although there are some strong arguments against the many-worlds picture of quantum mechanics, the reasons in favor are impressive as well. My own paper on many-worlds is an argument against it, so I'm hardly a partisan, but still I would give it 30 or 40 percent odds of turning out to be true.

I don't often stop to consider just how disquieting reality would be, if we do in fact occupy one of these "many worlds." As he often does, Chiang has teased out some disturbing implications of real science.

He does this by introducing a fantastical piece of technology to illustrate those implications. In the real world (or the real *worlds*, if many-worlds is correct) a "prism" permitting communication between branches could not exist. But Chiang accurately portrays how things would be if it did exist.

I have a bunch of thoughts about this story. I'm going to start with the science—I'll first prise apart the core of accurate (if speculative) physics

D. Baker (✉)
Ann Arbor, MI, USA
e-mail: djbaker@umich.edu

from the handful of places where the story takes a bit of dramatic license. Then I'll present an argument that the problem with free will in a branching universe is worse than Chiang's characters think it is. I also have some miscellaneous observations that I hope will be interesting; I'll clump these together at the end of the piece.

2.1 The Science

The central hypothesis of many-worlds quantum mechanics is illustrated faithfully in "Anxiety." If the theory is true, the whole of reality (all branches) is mathematically represented by a universal wavefunction. When the structure of this function is examined, we find that it contains many parts that behave like classical worlds—worlds in which Newton's physics does a pretty good job of describing how matter moves around. These are called branches.

When someone in one of these branches measures a property of a subatomic particle, a process called *decoherence* splits that branch into multiple branches. There will be at least one world for each possible outcome of the experiment (although the exact number of worlds is a thorny question as we'll see). In each branch is a new copy of every person from the original branch, including the experimenter. Each copy has the same memories as the original experimenter, and each feels like they are the same person as the original. This creates the illusion of randomness: because different copies see different results, it looks to the copies as if there was no way to predict how the experiment would turn out.

None of this is made up by Chiang—it might all be true, although there is no scientific consensus as yet. His one piece of dramatic license takes the form of the *prism*, a piece of technology that performs a measurement, generating two new branches, and sets up a line of communication between them.

The only connection between different branches is the extremely low level of interference that still exists after decoherence. In principle, an unimaginably advanced technology could measure this interference and collect information about other branches. But the technology required would be *godlike*, and such technology would be capable of detecting many different branches, not just specific ones that had recently branched off from our own.

A question of further interest is what sort of modifications to many-worlds would be required to allow prisms. In particular, we can ask how best to imagine the way the technology would work given the logic of branching worlds.

Suppose Prism A is activated on Monday. Then on Tuesday we have two branches, which we can call Branch A1 and Branch A2. The copy of Prism A in A1 can communicate with the copy of Prism A in A2.

On Wednesday, Prism B is then activated in both A1 and A2. We now have four branches: Branch A1 turns into A1B1 and A1B2, while Branch A2 becomes A2B1 and A2B2. The natural thing to say here is that Branch A1B1 can communicate with A2B1 but not A2B2. (Instead, Branch A2B2 becomes connected to Branch A1B2.)

The tricky question is what happens when Prism B is activated in Branch A1 on Wednesday, but not in Branch A2. It seems natural to say that we then have three branches: A1B1, A1B2 and A2. But then which branch on the "A1 side" of the tree gets to communicate with A2 using Prism A? (They can't both communicate with A2, since that would mean Prism A in A2 would be getting transmissions from two different paraselves, which is not what we see in the story!)

I take it that what's going on—what's implicit in the story, but not discussed explicitly to avoid confusing the reader—is that Branch A2 has to split as well whenever Branch A1 does, as long as Prism A is still working. So when Prism B is activated in Branch A1, Branch A2 splits along with A1. We end up with A1B1, A1B2, A2B1 and A2B2, just like before. The difference is that A2B1 and A2B2 don't have a way to communicate, since Prism B wasn't activated in those branches. So the people in A2B2 go on talking to A1B2, unaware that the people in A2B1 are having conversations (and perhaps very different conversations) with the people in A1B1.

This all makes internal sense, once we've added prisms to the physics of many-worlds. Normally goings-on in one branch would not cause branching in a different branch. Regular many-worlds quantum mechanics says that's impossible. But activating a prism in another branch that is linked to ours by a prism seems like exactly the sort of thing that would set off decoherence.

If I may editorialize for a moment, this gets to one of Chiang's remarkable gifts as a writer—he has an excellent sense for the intangible "feel" of scientific theories. In "Anxiety" (as in other works like "Story of Your Life") he constructs fictionalized science that is based off real science, and convincingly so, so that it *feels* like real science to the scientifically literate reader. It's the exact opposite of campy Star Trek technobabble.[1]

I've been going on as if it's meaningful to talk about the "number" of branches in the universal wavefunction. In fact this isn't really possible to make rigorous sense of this notion.

Consider a swimming pool containing water that's really churned up—maybe there's a lot of human activity in the pool or a hard rainstorm. How many waves or ripples are there in the pool? It depends on what standard you set for when one wave ends and the next one begins, or how high above a flat surface something needs to be to count as a wave. (Surely a few molecules rising above the surface isn't enough to make a wave.)

Something very similar applies to the question of how many branches there are in the many-worlds universal wavefunction. When does one branch end and another begin? It's a matter of how much *interference* exists between those two portions of the quantum wave. Interference is what makes quantum mechanical effects measurable. On the many-worlds picture, if there's too much interference between two branches they will be highly causally connected to each other—they won't really be separate branches at all. But there's always at least a tiny bit of interference between any two parts of the wavefunction.

This means that when Kevin wonders whether "being a jerk in this branch increase[s] the percentage of jerkish behavior across all branches," we need to understand the "percentage of branches" in an unconventional way. It doesn't make sense to count the number of jerkish branches and divide that by the total number of branches, since these aren't meaningful numbers. Instead, we must assume that the intensity of the wavefunction—the quantum *amplitude*—should be treated as if it measured the number of branches for each outcome.

But why should that be right, when there is no such thing as the number of branches? This is one of the toughest puzzles we run into in trying to understand many-worlds. I don't have a good answer, although many others have argued for their own solutions.

---

[1] No insult to Star Trek is intended here! Anyone acquainted with my aesthetic tastes would tell you that I adore camp.

2.2 Free Will?

Chiang treats human decisions as relatively predictable, fairly uniform between similar branches, and assumes that our decisions don't directly cause branching. I'm not sure if this is correct—and if it isn't correct, the implications for human free will are significant.

It may be that human decisions are chaotic systems. Chiang gives us a helpful example himself in his discussion of the weather. A chaotic system, like the weather, is highly sensitive to initial conditions. This means that a difference in a small part of the system can lead to big changes in large parts of it. It wouldn't surprise me at all if human cognition and decision-making counted as chaotic, although this question has not been studied and probably couldn't be answered with present technology.

If human decision-making *is* chaotic, this means that in many-worlds, our decisions will lead to branching. When Dana decides whether to betray Vinessa, for example, the world will split into branches where she betrays her and other branches where she acts loyally.

This is because chaos begets decoherence, and decoherence begets branching. Remember that decoherence happens when the properties of a quantum object like a small particle start to matter to the properties of a large object like a cloud or a human being. This is why performing a measurement leads to decoherence—the measurement device is a large object whose state depends in a sensitive way on a quantum object. For the same reason, a chaotic system like the weather doesn't just vary between branches, it *causes* branching (with different branches quickly developing different weather patterns).

I can't guarantee that the mind is a chaotic system that causes branching, but suppose it is. What becomes of the conclusion that Dana and her support group reach, that we have free will insofar as we may influence our future selves in many branches?

I'm afraid my own conclusions about free will in many-worlds are more pessimistic. I think it is plausible that our decisions do lead to branching. But this means we have no real control over our actions. Inevitably, when you choose to do the right thing, your parasélf—counterpart in another branch—will simultaneously choose to do the wrong thing.

Why should this branching decision pattern undermine free will? Here I will cite another insightful work of science fiction, Greg Egan's "Singleton" (Egan 2002). Egan portrays a scientist whose proudest moment is an act of heroism in which he ran to the aid of a man being brutally beaten. Later in life, the scientist comes to believe the many-worlds interpretation. He realizes that if his understanding of physics is correct, many of his other selves in other worlds must have succumbed to fear and left the man to his attackers.

Considering his daughter, he comes to believe that in an Everettian world it will be "impossible for her ever to act wholly in accordance with her ideals." And this, he thinks, would rob her of free will.

"Free will," Egan writes, "was a slippery notion, but to me it simply meant that your choices were more or less consistent with your nature" (Egan 2002). This is essentially what ethicists call the *deep self view* of free will, and it is perhaps the most common conception of how free will might be compatible with scientific determinism. And it would seem to require that we actually, reliably, behave in ways that accord with our individual natures, if we are to count as free.

But if your *nature* is to split into multiple copies whenever you face a tough decision, in what sense could we say that you are a good person or a bad one? In any given branch you'll behave well or badly, to be sure. But if we could see your behavior across all of the branches where copies of you exist, we would be hard pressed to say that a consistent, coherent personality has reliable control over your decisions.

This is the real threat to free will in the many-worlds interpretation.

2.3 Econ 10101010101010101

One of the most fascinating aspects of this story is the economic dimension. Chiang is clear that they haven't developed a way to "send money" across branches. But I wonder if he's too pessimistic about the prospects for cross-branch trade and division of labor.

Of course there would be no way to send material goods. So such trade would have to proceed by exchange of intellectual property and white-collar labor. The problem is finding a way to enforce contracts across branches when you can't reach out and arrest someone for violating them.

You could have a "gift economy" in which people across branches incrementally exchange services and information purely voluntarily. This is essentially what's portrayed in the story when Morrow deals with his paraself. A less unsavory version of this sort of gift exchange would make left-anarchist types like Kim Stanley Robinson very happy.

That said, I think Chiang is too quick to dismiss the possibility of a real market economy that spans branches. It would have to begin with purely voluntary exchange. But willing participants could give their cross-branch trading partners leverage that would allow for enforcing deals. For instance, if I in my branch wanted to trade with you in your branch, we could exchange embarrassing or incriminating secrets (or perhaps important trade secrets) and thereby gain a means of punishing each other for breach of contract. A banking system for sensitive secrets might ensue as a secure vehicle for enforcement.

There are darker sides to this possibility, as well. A morally compromised individual like Morrow might worry that his paraselves—who know lots of incriminating secrets about him—might try to blackmail him across branches. Perhaps the symmetry of the situation would prevent this, since the blackmail could go both ways. But if the same prism found its way into his paraself's possession in one branch, and an enemy of his held it in his own branch, he'd have good reason to worry.

Another way prisms could profoundly affect the economy is by helping us to quantify risk more precisely. Investors, entrepreneurs and consumers put considerable thought into the risks that attend their choices. With prisms, we could better estimate the probability of uncertain events like a market crash. One could imagine this bringing greater stability to markets, if investors see their assets performing well in many different branches at once, reinforcing their confidence that the risk of investing is low. On the other hand, an unlikely market crash in one branch could lead to panic in "neighboring" branches and cause an unfortunate chain reaction.[2]

2.4 What Does It All Mean?

Philosophers have posed many other puzzles connecting the many-worlds theory to questions of value. For example: if many-worlds is true, there are an infinite number of people in the multiverse (including us and all of our paraselves). This would seem to mean that our actions in this branch can't materially affect the total amount of human happiness, any more than adding a finite number to an infinite number can increase the size of the infinite number.

---

[2] On a related note, as a scholar of nuclear deterrence, I would sleep better at night if I could verify that there were hundreds of other branches that had split off from ours at the beginning of the Ukraine war, and that none of them were branches where the war escalated to a nuclear war!

Does this mean our actions really make no difference in the big scheme of things? It's a worry that might arise anyway, if one takes account of the vastness of the universe even within a single branch. I'm inclined to say that human well-being is not like a number. But it's a question that certainly bears further thought.

Another question that's obsessed one of my students is whether the vast number of people who exist according to many-worlds is a reason to believe the theory. The more people exist, the more likely it is that one or more of them would find himself in the situation where I find myself, observing the things I observe. Does this mean my existence is a prediction that confirms many-worlds?

This interpretation of quantum mechanics opens up a vast number of questions. No single work could ever do justice to all of them. But "Anxiety is the Dizziness of Freedom" is remarkable in doing as perfect a job as one could of exploring the free will issue in the form of fiction. I doubt there is a better story about free will anywhere in the multiverse.

Reference

Egan, Greg. 2002. Singleton. *Interzone* 176. https://www.gregegan.net/MISC/SINGLETON/Singleton.html.

PART II

God

CHAPTER 3

Death, God, and Meaning in Ted Chiang's Stories

Kiki Berk

Ted Chiang's short stories are among the most thought-provoking works of science fiction published in the last few decades. This chapter focuses on the philosophical ideas in two of these stories: "Omphalos" (2019) and "Exhalation" (2008). "Omphalos" raises questions about the relationship between God and the meaning of life, while "Exhalation" raises questions about death and how we ought to respond to it. With the help of theories and concepts from contemporary philosophy, this chapter explores and analyzes what these two stories have to say about death, God, and the meaning of life.

3.1 "Omphalos": Meaning and God

Can life be meaningful only if God exists? This is the central question of "Omphalos," which means "center." The story takes place in a world where empirical science supports young-earth creationism, the view that

K. Berk (✉)
Manchester, NH, USA

Southern New Hampshire University, Manchester, NH, USA
e-mail: k.berk@snhu.edu

the universe was created by God roughly 8000 years ago. The inhabitants of this world are convinced that human life is at the center of that universe—both literally and figuratively. Its main character, an archeologist named Dr. Dorothea Morrell, comes across a forthcoming scholarly article that proves scientifically that Earth is *not* at the center of the universe. Instead, the article argues, Earth was created as a trial run for, or perhaps as a side effect of, the creation of a *different* inhabited planet, which *is* at the center of the universe. This means that the humans on Dorothea's planet are not the epitome of God's creation. After all, as Dorothea reflects, "if we take as our premise that humanity was the reason for creation, then that should be reflected in the skies above just as much as in the earth beneath our feet. If humanity is the central fact of the universe, if our species is the omphalos, then a close examination of the celestial sphere should confirm that privileged status."[1] When she learns that it does *not*, Dorothea experiences an existential crisis and needs to take a break from her work at the Arisona archaeological dig because it seems pointless: "What does this matter? Everything we're doing here is irrelevant."[2] Dorothea has become convinced that human life, in general, and her own life, in particular, is meaningless.

Dorothea's crisis seems to result from the fact that she (tacitly) accepts the following claim: (1) human life is meaningful only if the human race was created by God for a purpose. Before her existential crisis, Dorothea also believed that (2) the human race was created by God for a purpose. The combination of these two views, (1) and (2), is called "supernaturalism." So, before her existential crisis, Dorothea was a *supernaturalist* about meaning. After she reads the article, however, she loses her belief in (2), i.e., that God created the human race (at least on *her* planet) for a purpose.[3] And since she still (tacitly) believes (1), she concludes that life is

---

[1] Chiang (2019: 265).

[2] Chiang (2019: 264).

[3] One could argue that the inhabitants of Omphalos were (or at least could have been) created for a purpose, namely, as a trial run for the planet which is at the center of the universe. But that would not be the *right kind* of purpose. In his classic paper "The Absurd," Thomas Nagel argues that not just any kind of purpose would make our lives meaningful. "If we learned that we were being raised to provide food for other creatures fond of human flesh, who planned to turn us into cutlets before we got too stringy – even if we learned that the human race had been developed by animal breeders precisely for this purpose – that would still not give our lives meaning" (Nagel 1971: 721). The same would be true of the inhabitants of Omphalos, if they were created as a trial run for another planet.

meaningless. This view—that life is meaningless—is called "nihilism." So, at this point in the story, Dorothea is a *nihilist* about meaning.

When Dorothea learns the truth about her world, she despairs. But she eventually finds a way out of her existential crisis. How? Not by convincing herself that God *did* create the humans on her planet for a purpose, but rather by rejecting the other component of supernaturalism—the claim that *human life is meaningful only if the human race was created by God for a purpose*.[4] Dorothea realizes that humans have always associated the *origin* of their species with its *value*, but that was wrong. As she puts it: "We have always seen it [i.e., evidence of creationism] as determinative of the value of our lives, but that wasn't inevitable. We chose to do that, which means we can choose to do otherwise."[5] When asking about the meaning of life, we shouldn't look at the origin of the world or of human life for an answer. Life can be meaningful even if it wasn't created for a purpose. This theory—that life can be meaningful in the absence of a God or a purpose for the human race—is called "naturalism." At the end of the story, Dorothea is a *naturalist* about meaning. This theory of meaning seems to be the one for which the story "Omphalos" ultimately advocates.

In the absence of a purpose given to it by God, what makes human life meaningful? More specifically, what makes *Dorothea's* life meaningful? Dorothea reflects on the fact that she has always found great satisfaction in being a scientist. While she became an archaeologist to discover God's purpose for the human race, the fact that no such purpose exists does not, she thinks, render her own scientific endeavors any less fulfilling. She concludes that she doesn't need God or a purpose to have meaning in her life. As she explains:

> I've devoted my life to studying the wondrous mechanism that is the universe, and doing so has given me a sense of fulfillment. I've always assumed that this meant that I was acting in accordance with your will, Lord, and your reason for making me. But if it's in fact true that you have no purpose in mind for me, then that sense of fulfillment has arisen solely from within myself. What that demonstrates to me is that we as humans are capable of creating meaning for our own lives.[6]

---

[4] In fact, many nihilists accept this claim as well. The difference between these nihilists and supernaturalists is that the former deny (whereas the latter accept) that God exists and created the human race for a purpose.
[5] Chiang (2019: 269).
[6] Chiang (2019: 269).

Dorothea seems to be saying that the fulfillment she experiences in her life as a scientist is enough to make her life meaningful, and this fulfillment comes entirely from herself, not from God.

The idea that she can feel fulfillment in her life without believing that God created the human race for a purpose pulls Dorothea out of her existential crisis. But is this a *good* account of meaning in life? That depends. Dorothea might be arguing that her life is meaningful simply because it *feels* meaningful. This view is called "subjective naturalism," and it holds that a person's life is meaningful if, and only if, she finds it meaningful. This view isn't very plausible. For one thing, a person can find her life meaningful while doing things that are clearly meaningless (e.g., counting blades of grass, collecting rubber bands, etc.); and for another, a person can arguably have a meaningful life even if she doesn't find it meaningful (e.g., a depressed surgeon who devotes her life to helping other people but can't see the purpose of or value in what she does).

Subjective naturalism is contrasted with objective naturalism, the view that a person must engage in projects that are objectively valuable (i.e., valuable in themselves) in order for that person's life to be meaningful. Although engaging in scientific discovery seems to be intrinsically valuable, it's unclear whether this is what Dorothea has in mind. After all, in her defense of what makes her own life worth living, she doesn't refer to the value of doing science for its own sake. But perhaps, one could argue, this is *implicit* in what she says. In other words, perhaps Dorothea is arguing that practicing science is meaningful because she finds it fulfilling *and* it's the sort of thing that is worthy of giving fulfillment. This version of naturalism is known as "hybrid naturalism," and its best-known proponent is Susan Wolf. According to Wolf, "meaning arises when subjective attraction meets objective attractiveness."[7] So, perhaps Dorothea is a hybrid naturalist, not a subjective naturalist. And in that case, her view of meaning is much more plausible.

There is, however, another interpretation of what Dorothea thinks makes her own life meaningful after she loses her belief that God created the humans on her planet for a purpose. After stating at the very end of the story that she is returning to the Arisona dig to continue her work in archeology, Dorothea declares: "This search [for *how* the universe operates] is my purpose; not because you chose it for me, Lord, but because I

---

[7] Wolf (1997: 224).

chose it for myself."⁸ Here, Dorothea appears to be saying that her work as a scientist is meaningful simply because she chooses to do it. Satisfaction does not even enter into the picture. The simple fact that she chooses to do this work is what makes it, and by extension her life, meaningful. This is reminiscent of the views of the twentieth-century French existentialist philosophers Simone de Beauvoir and Jean-Paul Sartre, who believe that nothing is inherently meaningful; things are meaningful only if we choose to pursue them and *in virtue of* our choosing to pursue them. These existentialist philosophers would say that Dorothea's scientific endeavors are meaningful simply because she chooses to do them—end of story. If this, and not a feeling of satisfaction or a recognition of intrinsic value, is why Dorothea thinks that her own life as meaningful, then she is, at bottom, an existentialist about meaning in life.⁹

3.2 "Exhalation": Living in the Face of Death

How should we live in the face of death? In his story "Exhalation," Ted Chiang thoughtfully engages this question by imagining a species of seemingly immortal conscious machines, one of which discovers the source of life and the fact that its kind isn't truly immortal after all. Interested in how memory works, the nameless narrator self-dissects its own brain and discovers that its memories are just patterns of air directed by thousands of tiny gold-leaf switches. The same is true of its other mental states, including its consciousness, thoughts, and personality. The narrator's species has always assumed that air is the source of life, which is why individual machines take such great care to replace their own "lungs" (tanks of compressed air) before they run out. But the narrator's self-dissection experiment shows that the source of life isn't air itself but rather a difference in air pressure. Around the same time, and through different means, the narrator discovers that the air pressure in its universe is slowly decreasing, which will eventually result in the death of its entire species. Up to that point death was possible but uncommon; now it seems to be inevitable. As a species, the machines are forced to come to terms with their own

---

⁸ Chiang (2019: 269).

⁹ How the existentialist theory of meaning relates to the other theories of meaning discussed earlier is a hard question. Existentialists are often characterized as subjective naturalists, but I think there are good reasons to resist this interpretation. For more on this issue, see Berk (2022).

mortality. The initial reaction is "widespread panic," but that settles down once they learn that universal death is still a few centuries off. "In the meantime," the narrator tells us, "there is much discussion over how we should spend the time that remains to us."[10] The narrator goes on to discuss three possibilities—i.e., three ways of living in the face of death.

The first way is a form of radical resistance or non-acceptance. In the story, a sect called "the Reversalists" is formed, and it tries to restore the disequilibrium of air pressure, which would save the machines' lives. While their various attempts to do this fail, they remain undeterred. The Reversalists in the machine world can be compared to the Transhumanists in our own. The latter, of which Ray Kurzweil is the best-known member, advocate for the enhancement of human beings, including the eradication of aging and death. Instead of seeing them as inevitable natural processes, Transhumanists regard aging and death as preventable malfunctions akin to illness and disease. And even though they haven't yet succeeded, Transhumanists have invested millions of dollars into the development of technologies that delay aging, extend life, and eliminate death. Some believers, for whom this technology would come too late, have had their bodily remains frozen through cryogenics in the hopes of being resurrected when such technology (hopefully) exists.

The second way of living in the face of death focuses on surviving death in a metaphorical way. This is sometimes called "pseudo-immortality" because the individuals who "live on" in this sense do not literally survive death. Rather, such people "live on" in the thoughts and memories of others. Even though this might seem to provide little solace for death (as Woody Allen put it: "I don't want to live on in the hearts of my countrymen, I want to live on in my apartment"), it's still a source of hope, motivation, and comfort for many people. Part of the reason why we do such things as write books and have children is to leave behind a trace of ourselves after we are gone. In "Exhalation," the narrator hopes for a kind of pseudo-immortality. It hopes that explorers will someday discover its world and read its account. This, the narrator says, would be a way of surviving death: "And in that way I live again, through you."[11]

A third way of living in the face of death is to reflect on our own mortality in order to better appreciate our lives while we still have them. The narrator, speaking directly to the reader, assumes that the reader is mortal,

---

[10] Chiang (2019: 52).
[11] Chiang (2019: 56).

too, and aware of their own mortality. It goes on to say that it hopes that the reader is "not saddened by that awareness."[12] Why not? Because life, and the variety of wonderful things that life has created—including architecture, art, music, and poetry—didn't have to be here at all. "Our universe might have slid into equilibrium emitting nothing more than a quiet hiss. The fact that it spawned such plenitude is a miracle, one that is matched only by your universe giving rise to you."[13] Our lives and the world around us may not strike us as being miraculous, but they are. And we, like the narrator in the story, can come to see this through a confrontation with our own mortality. This, then, is how we should live in the face of death according to the narrator, who ends its account with the following valediction: "Contemplate the marvel that is existence, and rejoice that you are able to do so."[14] In short, a confrontation with death might open our eyes to a new way of living: living in awareness of the miracle that life truly is.

While "Exhalation" considers three different ways of living in the face of death, it is this third way—reflecting on one's own mortality in order to better appreciate life—for which the story ultimately advocates. But is this response really superior to the other two? The story doesn't offer any arguments in favor of its preferred response, but I can think of two: one practical, one philosophical. Practically, this response is more under an individual's own control than the other two. Whether Transhumanists will succeed in defeating biological death is anyone's guess, and whether anyone will remember us after we die is more up to other people than it is up to us. By contrast, each of us has complete control over how much we appreciate the marvel of being alive. Second, and more philosophically, this response is grounded in an acceptance of mortality, whereas the other two responses can be seen as forms of denial. There is a tension between trying to live forever, either literally or metaphorically, and accepting the fact that one is going to die. Since acceptance is preferable to denial, it follows that accepting our own mortality, and making the most of the lives we have, is preferable to trying to live forever—either literally (through not dying) or metaphorically (in the minds of others).

---

[12] Chiang (2019: 56).
[13] Chiang (2019: 57).
[14] Chiang (2019: 57).

3.3 Conclusion

"Omphalos" and "Exhalation" are profound stories that address some of the deepest questions that human beings can ask. What is the meaning of life? Does the meaning of life depend on God? How should we live in the face of death? According to "Exhalation," reflecting on our own mortality can help us better appreciate life by allowing us to see it for the miracle it is. According to "Omphalos," God is not necessary for individual lives to be meaningful; rather, we can create our own meaning by choosing to pursue things that we find fulfilling. The central message of both stories is thus an empowering one: it's part of the human condition to live without God and in the face of death, but this need not sadden us or prevent us from living meaningful lives.

References

Berk, Kiki. 2022. Why Beauvoir Is Not a Subjectivist about Meaning in Life. *Journal of Philosophy of Life* 12 (1): 39–54.
Chiang, Ted. 2019. *Exhalation*. New York: Vintage Books.
Nagel, Thomas. 1971. The Absurd. *Journal of Philosophy* 68 (20): 716–727.
Wolf, Susan. 1997. Happiness and Meaning: Two Aspects of the Good Life. *Social Philosophy and Policy* 12 (1): 207–225.

CHAPTER 4

The Presence of Evil and the Absence of God

Bradley Rettler

4.1 Introduction

Angelic visitations in our world are at best rare, and at worst they never occur at all. Not so in Neil Fisk's world. There, angelic visitations are common—and often deadly. Neil lost his wife to such a visitation, and he's hated God ever since. The problem with this hatred is that Neil is quite sure his wife is in heaven, as he saw her soul ascending and has never seen her walking around in hell during the frequent glimpses the living are given of the underworld. Since Neil thinks he cannot willingly become devout, he must rely on a divine glitch; those who are caught in heaven's light during an angelic visitation involuntarily become devout and thus go to heaven. Luckily for Neil, he drives into a beam of heaven's light, loses his sight, and becomes devout. Unluckily for Neil, God sends him to hell anyway.

B. Rettler (✉)
University of Wyoming, Laramie, WY, USA
e-mail: brettler@uwyo.edu

© The Author(s), under exclusive license to Springer Nature
Switzerland AG 2025
D. Friedell (ed.), *The Philosophy of Ted Chiang*,
https://doi.org/10.1007/978-3-031-81662-8_4

In the story notes, Ted Chiang says that he wrote the story "thinking about the problem of innocent suffering",[1] and in an interview about the story, he says, "there are people who are also frustrated by the problem of innocent suffering, while still feeling a strong belief in God. That seems to me to be a difficult position to be in. Which is what 'Hell is the Absence of God' is all about."[2]

This is a familiar theme; nearly everyone has at some point considered some version of the argument from evil against the existence of God. The simplest version is that a good God wouldn't allow evil, so there must not be a God. A more complicated but more precise version goes like this: a morally perfect being would want to prevent any evil that it knows about and can stop. An all-powerful being can stop any evil that it knows about. And an all-knowing being knows about all the evil. So, if God is all-knowing, all-powerful, and morally perfect, then God knows about all evil and can stop it and would stop it. But there's evil. So either God isn't all-knowing, or God isn't all-powerful, or God isn't morally perfect—or there is no God at all.

The argument from evil is the most well-known argument against the existence of God. But it's not the only one. The argument from evil points out one feature of the world—the existence of evil—that seems incompatible with, or at least evidence against, the existence of God. But there may well be other features of the world that also seem incompatible with the existence of God.

One such feature is people who don't believe in God. Presumably God cares whether people believe that God exists. And if God exists, God knows who doesn't believe, and has enough power to give those people incontrovertible proof of God's existence. For example, God could visit them and have a conversation, perform miracles, and repeat this as many times as it takes. Or perhaps God could write in the sky, "I AM THE LORD YOUR GOD." God would know, for each nonbeliever, exactly what it would take to convince them.

But God doesn't do that. Nonbelievers abide. And many are nonbelievers, not due to any hostility or incorrigibility but solely due to the lack of evidence they have of God's existence. Bertrand Russell, author of *Why I Am Not a Christian*, was once asked in an interview what he would say if, after his death, he appeared before God in heaven. He responded, "I

---

[1] Chiang (2010, p. 273).
[2] Grant (2009).

probably would ask, 'Sir, why did you not give me better evidence?'"[3] Whether or not Russell himself would have believed in God if he had more evidence, there seem to be many people who would.

4.2 Hiddenness and Evil

One can read "Hell is the Absence of God" as a story about the problem of evil. I read it as a story about the problem of hiddenness. And I think it's more interesting to think about it through that lens. After all, we're familiar with much of the suffering in the story—physical injury, loss of life, divorce, loss of hope, and so on. But the evidence of God's existence provided to those in the story is very different from what we experience. In the story, God is not hidden. Chiang doesn't mention atheists or agnostics, but it's not a stretch to imagine that there aren't any—that nobody in the story doesn't believe that God exists. And yet clearly there are plenty who aren't devout, in Chiang's words, which I take to be something like "have a positive attitude toward God". That's a category that very few people in our world, if any, occupy—believers in God but not fans of God. Usually people who aren't fans of God think that there is no God and that it would be pretty bad if there were a God. And most people who believe in God are (or try to be) devout to some degree.

Some people think that the argument from hiddenness is just a version of the argument from evil. They say that one of the unfortunate things about the world—one of the evils—is that God is not forthcoming with evidence for God's existence. But this is a mistake. If everyone believed in God, for example, then there'd be no need for God to provide all this extra evidence. Such a lack of evidence wouldn't be evil.

There are more reasons to think the arguments are independent. Peter van Inwagen, in his "What is the Problem of Divine Hiddenness?", imagines a world without any evil.[4] Nobody suffers for longer than a few minutes, and anyone who suffers is rewarded immediately with goods that far outweigh the suffering. Such a world is possible. There is no contradiction in supposing that a world is this way. And in such a world, there is no argument from evil. Recall that one of the premises of the argument from evil is there is suffering. And in this imagined world, there is no suffering.

---

[3] Rosten (1974).
[4] van Inwagen (2002).

But, says van Inwagen, that doesn't mean that everyone in our imagined world believes in God. Add to our imagined world that God doesn't provide much—if any—evidence of God's existence. There may well be nonbelievers. Their doubts about God's existence are not due to the argument from evil; instead, they don't believe in God for the same reason that I don't believe there's a perfectly cooked steak in the next room—there's no evidence for it.

So, van Inwagen's described world has hiddenness, but no suffering. The fact that we can imagine such a world is a good reason to think that the argument from evil is distinct from the argument from hiddenness. Chiang's world, by contrast, has evil but no hiddenness. Angels regularly visit and proclaim God's glory. However, there is suffering. Indeed, there is suffering brought about by those very angelic visitations! Chiang's story thereby gives us another reason to think that the argument from evil is distinct from the argument from hiddenness.

4.3 Responses to the Argument from Hiddenness

To respond to the argument from hiddenness, theists usually seek to offer justifying reasons or compensating goods for God's failure to provide sufficient evidence to everyone. An attempt to offer a justifying reason for God remaining hidden is an attempt to state what bad outcome God's hiddenness avoids or an attempt to explain why God must remain hidden. For example, a justifying reason for the pain I experience at the dentist is that I would experience even worse pain without the procedure, but if the dentist causes more pain than is necessary to avoid that worse pain, they've done something wrong. An attempt to offer a compensating good for God remaining hidden is an attempt to state what good outcome results from God's being hidden that wouldn't have resulted otherwise. For example, a compensating good for my being gone from my children is the money I get paid to work, which I use to buy food and housing; I wouldn't get that money if I didn't leave the house to work.

I'll briefly cover some justifying reasons and compensating goods on offer, and then suggest a new one that I think Chiang's story helps us to see. I won't be evaluating the competitors—just discussing them.

One example of a justifying reason on offer is God's personality.[5] Perhaps what we take to be silence is actually just God interacting with us

---

[5] Rea (2011) and (2018, especially ch 5).

in the way God prefers. Perhaps God prefers communion to communication, as Rea puts it (2011, p. 273). And of course, it's a very great good for God to act out God's personality.[6]

Another justifying reason is that God wants to avoid people being devout for the wrong reasons.[7] Travis Dumsday (2014) suggests that if God were to give more evidence—evidence sufficient for everyone to believe—then many people might believe simply because they are overawed by the experience of God and not because they've carefully thought through God's nature. And Howard-Snyder (1996 and 2016) suggests that if God shows too much power there may be many people who become devout out of a self-interested motivation to be on the winning side; they'd be treating God as a means to an end, and not loving God for the right reasons.

An example of a compensating good is free will.[8] If God were to overwhelm us with evidence, says this response, we could not freely respond. Our response would be coerced.[9] And so God must give us an amount of evidence that allows us to exercise free will in responding. A related compensating good is faith.[10] Faith, the response says, is required for salvation. And faith requires lack of knowledge or lack of certainty. Neither of these are compatible with God providing enough evidence to convince all nonbelievers.

And then there's a special kind of response: skeptical theism, which offers neither a justifying reason nor a compensating good.[11] Instead, the skeptical theist says that we should not expect to find one at all! We have, the skeptical theist says, no reason to think that if God were to have a justifying reason or compensating good for allowing nonbelievers, we would know what it is and recognize it as such. After all, God is much smarter than us and knows the nonbelievers' mental states much better than we do, and so we shouldn't expect to know the justifying reasons or compensating goods God might be thinking of when choosing to stay hidden.

---

[6] I am working (with Andrew M. Bailey) on a book on how thinking about God as having a personality affects arguments in the philosophy of religion, including evil, hiddenness, salvation, the Principle of Sufficient Reason, and so on. See Bailey and Rettler (2024).
[7] Dumsday (2014) and Howard Snyder (1996 and 2016).
[8] As in Hick (1966) and Swinburne (1998).
[9] See Murray (1993).
[10] See Dumsday (2014).
[11] See, e.g., Howard-Snyder (2016) and McBrayer and Swenson (2012).

4.4 A New Response

I think Chiang's story provides another response to the argument from hiddenness in the form of a justifying reason.

It's worth thinking more carefully about what kind of evidence the people in the story have. Does everyone in the world of the story really have decisive evidence of God's existence? Consider whether they might have some questions, even after coming to know that God exists. For example, they might wonder why God sends angels, and why the appearances of angels result in so much death and destruction. Could the angels not have come in a more peaceful way? Could they not have provided evidence of God's existence and delivered God's message in a nonlethal manner? Neither the angels nor God answers those questions in the story. But even supposing God or the angels did, people might have follow-up questions about those answers. And so on.

I think the upshot is this: perhaps the justifying reason for divine hiddenness is that it's impossible to get decisive evidence that God exists.

Certainly, the people in the story get evidence of *something*. There are mighty beings that appear out of thin air, radiate power, announce God's glory, miraculous things happen, and then they disappear. Heaven's light shines on people who then become devout. Scientists in this world presumably have no natural explanation for these occurrences, and so these occurrences are supernatural. But does that mean they're *divine*? If the explanation is not natural, must it be *God*?

When we use the term "God" in philosophy of religion, we don't use it as a name for a person but rather as a shorthand for a description, since atheists can make claims about God while not believing there's any such person. The description at least includes "is a being that is all-knowing, all-powerful, and morally perfect". Any being that lacks any of these characteristics simply isn't God. So, according to this understanding, we could find out that God didn't create the world or that God didn't have a son named Jesus, since creating the world and having a son named Jesus aren't part of the description, but we couldn't find out that God occasionally does morally bad things, since being morally perfect is essential.

We can say that, despite all the angels, God is hidden in Neil's world, because the evidence of God's existence doesn't settle that God is all-knowing, all-powerful, and morally perfect. Neil may well wonder whether God is morally perfect, given that sending the angel Nathanael caused Neil's wife to die. Neil may also wonder whether God is all-knowing, given that God seems unaware of what's happening in hell. Neil may wonder whether God is all-powerful, given that the angels seem unable to announce God's glory without accompanying devastation. And what goes for Neil goes for the rest of his world. It seems a perfectly natural response to wonder whether the being sending all the angels really is morally perfect. And with all the reasonable doubt, it's not obvious that devotion is the right attitude to take toward the angel-sender.

Let's take it one step further. *We* may wonder whether Chiang is accurate in describing the angel-sender as God, given these reasons to doubt the angel-sender's moral perfection! Chiang has named the being "God", but given that *we're* using God as a description for an all-knowing, all-powerful, and morally perfect being, we may well wonder whether Chiang's God fits our description of God. Perhaps this is a world in which there is no God, but a very powerful chaotic neutral or chaotic evil being.

This new response denies the premise of the argument from hiddenness that says that God would provide sufficient evidence of God's existence; according to the new response, this is impossible. Even in a world like the one Chiang describes, there are people who are not devout because God has not revealed *enough*. And for all we know, God can never reveal enough.

No matter how much power a being displays, it can't prove it has infinite power. No matter how much good a being does, it can't prove it's morally perfect. Even if the being in question is God. Indeed, given all God's knowledge, it's not at all surprising to think that a morally perfect God would appear to us to be morally imperfect, since we can't see all the justifying reasons and compensating goods for evil.

In that respect, this response to the argument from hiddenness pairs nicely with skeptical theism as a response to the argument from evil. Given the amount and variety of evil and the gap in knowledge between God and us, we have no reason to think that if God were to have a justifying reason or compensating good for allowing suffering, we would know what it is and recognize it as such. And because of this, God can never give us sufficient evidence of God's moral perfection.

Acknowledgments Thanks to Andrew M Bailey, David Friedell, Hannah Kim, Rylan Knopp, Steve Rettler, and Laura Warmke for helpful comments.

REFERENCES

Bailey, Andrew, & Bradley Rettler. 2024. *The Problem of Divine Personality.* Cambridge University Press.

Chiang, Ted. 2010. *Stories of Your Life and Others.* Small Beer Press.

Dumsday, Travis. 2014. Divine Hiddenness and the Opiate of the People. *International Journal for Philosophy of Religion* 76 (2): 193–207.

Grant, Gavin J. 2009. Ted Chiang: Interviewed by Gavin J. Grant. IndieBound. Archived from the original on February 11, 2009. Retrieved October 10, 2023 from https://web.archive.org/web/20170407032812/http://www.indiebound.org/author-interviews/chiangted.

Hick, J. 1966. Evil and the God of Love. Macmillan.

Howard-Snyder, Daniel. 1996. The Argument from Divine Hiddenness. *Canadian Journal of Philosophy* 26 (3): 433–453.

———. 2016. Divine Openness and Creaturely Non-Resistant Non-Belief. In *Hidden Divinity and Religious Belief: New Perspectives*, ed. Eleonore Stump and Adam Green, 126–138. Cambridge University Press.

van Inwagen, Peter. 2002. What Is the Problem of the Hiddenness of God? In *Divine Hiddenness: New Essays*, ed. Daniel Howard-Snyder and Paul Moser, 24–32. New York: Cambridge University Press.

McBrayer, Justin P. & Swenson, P. 2012. Scepticism about the argument from divine hiddenness. *Religious Studies* 48(2): 129–150.

Murray, Michael. 1993. Coercion and the Hiddenness of God. *American Philosophical Quarterly* 30 (1): 27–38.

Rea, Michael C. 2011. Divine Hiddenness, Divine Silence. In *Philosophy of Religion: An Anthology*, ed. Louis P. Pojman and Michael C. Rea, 266–275. Wadsworth/Cenage.

———. 2018. *The Hiddenness of God.* New York: Oxford University Press.

Rosten, Leo. 1974. Bertrand Russell and God: A Memoir. *The Saturday Review*: 25–26.

Swinburne, Richard. 1998. *Providence and the Problem of Evil.* Oxford University Press UK.

CHAPTER 5

Mysterious Ways: Making Sense of God's Actions in *Hell Is the Absence of God*

Gabriel Oak Rabin

Upon reading *Hell Is the Absence of God*, the philosophical issue that most readily comes to mind is the problem of evil, which goes something like this.[1] If God exists, he is good, all-knowing, and all-powerful. A good, all-knowing, and all-powerful being would not permit unnecessary evil. But the world does contain unnecessary evil (e.g. the Holocaust). Therefore, God does not exist, is not good, is not all-knowing (and does not eliminate the Holocaust because he does not know about it), or is not all-powerful (and lacks the power to prevent the Holocaust). All of these options seem to go against the doctrines of many world religions. Rather than denying God's existence, goodness, knowledge, or power, the typical response of religious thinkers has been to deny that there is unnecessary evil. This is a tough row to hoe—it certainly seems like 1,000,000 fewer

---

[1] The problem of evil is old enough that it would be foolish to attribute it to any one thinker. David Hume (1779) discusses it in his *Dialogues Concerning Natural Religion*, but even he attributes the problem to Epicurus. The presentation here is heavily influenced by J.L. Mackie's (1955) "Evil and Omnipotence", which has informed much recent discussion.

G. O. Rabin (✉)
New York University Abu Dhabi, Abu Dhabi, UAE
e-mail: gabriel.oak.rabin@gmail.com

© The Author(s), under exclusive license to Springer Nature Switzerland AG 2025
D. Friedell (ed.), *The Philosophy of Ted Chiang*,
https://doi.org/10.1007/978-3-031-81662-8_5

deaths would have been less evil. But religious thinkers are forced into the uncomfortable position that 6,000,000 deaths was necessary; 5,000,000 wouldn't have been sufficient.

There are many responses to the problem of evil; I will not take the time to canvas them all here. Obviously much turns on what it takes for an evil to be "necessary". I actually think that *Hell Is the Absence of God* focuses not solely the problem of evil but on the slightly different problem of making sense of God's actions, and particularly God's system of *desert*. God is the ultimate judge, dispensing reward and punishment, in accordance with God's infinite wisdom, in both the mortal realm and the afterlife. But God is good, all-knowing, and all-powerful. Such a judge would reward only those who are deserving of reward and punish those who are deserving of punishment. More generally, all the actions of a wise and good being like God would make sense. This includes the dispensation of good as well as bad outcomes. And since God is all-powerful and created the universe, nearly every event that occurs is, ultimately, attributable to God. Thus the events of the world should make sense.

Typically, discussions of the problem of evil use the suffering *of innocents* as the paradigm of evil.[2] For example, children who die from painful illness. Or, at least, individuals whose small guilts do not merit the treatment they receive in the ovens of Dauchau. (It's worth remembering that some Christian theology holds that we are all guilty of "original sin". Thus, no one is innocent. Within this type of framework, one must shift focus to the claim that many who suffer are, rather than innocent, instead not guilty of crimes serious enough to merit the calamities that befall them). The evil here is that God seems to punish those who do not deserve it. We are thus faced with a version of the problem of making sense of God's actions and his system of desert.

There is a flip side to the suffering, or punishment, of the innocent: the rewarding of the guilty. Chiang's story contains a clear example. He discusses "the case of Barry Larsen, a serial rapist and murderer who, while disposing of the body of his latest victim, witnessed a visitation and was seen ascending to Heaven, much to the outrage of his victims' families"[3]

---

[2] Chiang himself, in his Story Notes, calls the issue at hand "the problem of innocent suffering." (280).

[3] One common response to those who worry about why God would permit the wicked to flourish is that the wicked will receive appropriate punishment in the afterlife. Interestingly, the case of Barry Larsen is immune this reply.

(2002, 226). This situation seems even farther removed from the problem of evil and fits much better in the framing of the issue as one of making sense of God's actions. The problem here is not the presence of evil, but really the lack of evil, or least punishment, laid onto Barry Larsen, a paradigm of someone worthy of God's punishment.[4] Here, Chiang is really laying the (at least seemingly) nonsensical nature of God's actions on thickly. Many inhabitants of the world of *Hell Is the Absence...* must, upon hearing the tale of Barry Larsen, have thought to themselves, "What was God thinking!?" The system of reward and punishment at play seems more like the whims of an irrational drunkard or, at best, an immature five-year-old.

The inclusion of the Barry Larsen example, as well as others, makes me less inclined to treat *Hell Is the Absence...* as a story about the problem of evil and more as a story about individual people trying to make sense of God's actions, particularly his system of reward and punishment.[5] Each of the protagonists grapples with this problem in their own way. The character Janice Reilly is crippled by God while still in the womb and thus seems to be unjustly punished. (It's hard to get more innocent than a fetus.) Later in life, Janice has the use of her legs restored. But that restoration disrupts her life and eventually she realizes that she does not want the use of her legs back. Janice is devout, so the restoration of her legs is not an undeserved reward *per se*. But she does not believe that this miracle is a reward at all. And she is doubly confused as to why God would both remove her legs and then later return them. She struggles to make sense

---

[4] One could attempt to fold this case, and perhaps all cases, into the umbrella of the problem of evil. Perhaps the fact that good, rather than bad, things happen to Barry Larsen, who is deserving of punishment, is itself an "evil" in some sense. Certainly miscarriages of justice do strike us as "evil" in some legitimate sense of that term. But I'm a bit loathe to call good events "evil". Doing so causes the nomenclature to get very tricky very quickly. It's also worth noting that the hedonist theory of utility, in particular, will actually have a very difficult time making sense of these claims. On that theory, the only intrinsic good is pleasure and only intrinsic bad is pain. Any addition of pleasure to the world, even the pleasure of a serial rapist and murderer, makes the world a better place. And hedonism is a popular theory of the good.

Here, I think it better to remain neutral. I don't want to get drawn into a discussion (or perhaps a territorial squabble) over whether every instance of making sense of God's actions, including the rewarding of the guilty, is a sub-category of the problem of evil. *Prima facie*, it seems like a different topic. We'll stick with that understanding.

[5] Bradley Rettler (2025), in this volume, also investigates *Hell Is the Absence* through the lens of an issue other than the problem of evil. He considers the problem of divine hiddenness.

of God's actions, and particularly God's actions toward her. Evil plays no salient role in Janice's intellectual struggle.

In sharp contrast to Janice Reilly, Ethan Mead feels that God has not intervened *enough* in his life. "Ever since childhood he'd felt certain that God had a special role for him to play, and he waited for a sign telling him what that role was" (214). For whatever reason, Ethan feels that he is due for a divine intervention. Eventually, he is present for a visitation by the angel Rashiel (the same visitation that restores Janice Reilly's legs). But nothing special happens to him. A crack opens up in the pavement in front of Ethan that "seemed to be pointing him in a specific direction" (215). But following the crack led to no illumination of God's special purpose for him. Ethan remains always "watchful for signs of a greater destiny" (214). As a reader, we can and should question Ethan's certainty that God has something special in mind for him. But Ethan lives in a world where God frequently intervenes. Sometimes in surprising and eyebrow-raising ways, by replacing the legs of fetus with flippers and pardoning serial rapists. Everyone who inhabits this world is faced full-on with the problem of making sense of God's actions. Ethan's response to the problem is to find God's purpose *for him*. But he remains perplexed: "everyone except Ethan had found a way to understand what had happened to them" (215). Ethan serves as a model for both those who yearn for a special relationship to God and those who remain perplexed by God's actions.

Lastly we turn to our protagonist, Neil Fisk. Neil is not particularly concerned with figuring out why God did or didn't do this or that. Neil certainly regrets the death of his wife Sarah, whom he loved dearly. But Neil's main concern is not deducing why God took his wife's life during a visit by the Angel Nathaneal. Instead, the animating dilemma that directs Neil's life is how he can be reunited with Sarah in the afterlife. He understands that "the only way to get to Heaven was to love God with all his heart" (209). But Neil can't bring himself to do that, despite his various attempts at different methods and arguments for conversion. Neil isn't the Wykeham Professor of Logic, but he is a rational man. Neil was not raised devout, so blind faith in and love of God is not an option for him. Neil needs a reason to love God. This is why he talks to so many different devout people, hoping that one of their arguments might convince him to love God. But these arguments all fail. It is worth asking why they fail. Perhaps the arguments simply aren't good enough. Any philosopher or priest can certainly relate to that: rarely are people, through argument, convinced to love God. Argument can do well rebutting criticisms or alleviating concerns of those who are already committed.[6] But generating full-on conversion is a difficult ask.

But the biggest part of the problem stares both the reader and Neil Fisk in the face: the God of *Hell Is the Absence of God* does not seem particularly worthy of love. Uncontroversially, God is powerful. He regularly causes earthquakes and bestows sight to the blind. But power alone does not make anyone worthy of love. If it did, we would all love Genghis Khan and Adolf Hitler. Great power is a double-edged sword. A capricious child is a nuisance. A capricious child holding an armed pistol is a crisis. A large part of Neil's problem is God's seemingly fickle behavior, which we have already discussed at length. Neil is not particularly interested in making sense of God's actions *per se*, because of his curiosity or the intrinsically interesting nature of the intellectual puzzle. Instead, Neil has the more mundane but completely relatable goal of reuniting with this wife. This goal can only be reached by loving God. But Neil can't make himself love God any more than he can make himself love a porcupine or believe that he was born in 1358. He needs *reasons*. Neil finds himself at the center of a maze. At the maze's end lies his wife, who can only be reached via the pathway of loving God. But the route from Neil's current mental state to loving God is long and confusing, and Neil can't see a way to get from here to there. God has made the maze particularly devious because of how difficult it is to make sense of his actions.

None of Janice, Ethan, or Neil are particularly concerned with the problem of evil. But they are all trying to make sense of God's actions, albeit for different reasons. The situation of these protagonists is mirrored, to some extent, by every person who inhabits the world of *Hell Is the Absence of God*. In that world, everyone, and not just the faithful, faces the problem of making sense of God's actions. In our world, atheists typically do not trouble themselves with God. Perhaps they reject his existence because of the problem of evil. But really the best evidence against the existence of God is simply the lack of evidence for it. Most do not believe in God for precisely the same reason they do not believe in invisible silent odorless gremlins in their attic: there is no evidence for it. But in the world of *Hell Is the Absence of God*, God is not a silent gremlin. He makes a lot of noise. He regularly interacts with the natural world in exactly the way

---

[6] Even the rich literature on the problem of evil is entirely a defensive maneuver: a discussion of how to rebut an argument *against* the existence of God. None of that discussion helps one to positively establish the existence of God or provide reasons for loving him.

the holy books say he would: by sending Angels to perform healing miracles accompanied by rays of heavenly light. In that world, atheism isn't really an option for the thinking person who is responsive to the evidence. The result of all this is that everyone, and not just the faithful, must grapple with the problem of making sense of God's actions.

In fact, the inhabitants of *Hell Is the Absence of God* must grapple with a more extreme version of the problem than we inhabitants of the actual world do. The world of *Hell Is the Absence of God* involves even *more* punishment of the innocent and rewarding of the guilty than our world does. And that punishment of innocent and rewarding of the guilty is *directly* traceable to God and his angelic agents. One common response to the problem of evil is "the free will defense", according to which the world's allegedly unnecessary evils are caused by the free actions of people.[7] Free will is a great good, but in giving people free will, God also gives them the power to do evil. But the benefit of free will is worth the cost of the evil thereby generated. Or so the free will defense claims. A similar response seems available for the more general problem of making sense of the world and God's actions: the seemingly nonsensical actions are the result of people's free will, and that free will is a good worth the cost of occasional nonsense. Unfortunately, this line of reasoning works poorly in *Hell Is the Absence of God*. In that world, much of the innocent suffering is caused directly by God (or at least by the angels who are his instruments) instead of being caused by free-willed people. By making God directly responsible for certain events, Chiang cleverly undercuts the free will defense.

Another response to the problem of evil, which works equally well for the problem of making sense of God's actions, is the "mysterious ways" response. This is the idea that God has his hidden reasons for tolerating, or even causing, the allegedly unnecessary evil we see in the world. The evil we see is, contrary to appearances, truly necessary. When people receive punishment (or reward) they seem not to deserve, this serves some greater purpose. God has his reasons, but we limited creatures do not understand them. (This is sometimes paired with the claim that we can never understand them, and other times paired with the claim that God's reasons will be revealed to us in the afterlife.) From our perspective, "the Lord works in mysterious ways".

---

[7] Alvin Plantinga's (1974) *God, Freedom, and Evil* offers the canonical version of the free will defense.

One problem with the "mysterious ways" defense is that it is unclear what purpose is served by God making his ways so opaque and hidden from us. Doing so makes it harder for us to believe in him and his goodness. (Here is where the claim that the explanation is beyond our human cognitive abilities is sometimes trotted in by the defense.) It is also worth noting that any human who acted in these ways—by punishing those who did not deserve it, bestowing favors upon those who did not want them, and causing unnecessary pain and suffering—we would call a madman. Never would we claim that this person was "working in mysterious ways" and deserved of our love, support, and worship. The fundamental problem with the "mysterious ways" response is that it has seemed, to many, not like a response to the problem but like the promise of a response. A promise that is never met, but that we are supposed to trust anyway.

Hell Is the Absence of God provides a *reductio* of the "God works in mysterious ways" response. Or, if not a full *reductio*, to at least cause proponents of that response to question *how much* nonsensical behavior they would tolerate on the part of this all-powerful lord before they retract their love and respect. Or at least to admit that God is either not perfectly good, not all-knowing, or not all-powerful. Maybe the interlocutor will stand their ground and claim that no amount of apparently ill or nonsensical treatment at the hands of God would cause them to reconsider.[8] Ironically, this is exactly the situation that the main protagonist Neil Fisk finds himself in at the end of the story.

Eventually, Neil attempts a risky path out of the maze, by exploiting what he takes to be a loophole in God's system of reward and punishment. The loophole is this: exposure to heaven's light causes anyone upon whom it shines to love God fully and unconditionally, and thus to be worthy of ascension to heaven upon death. (The existence of a loophole in the holy system of desert only adds to the problem of making sense of God.) Neil's chosen path is exceptionally risky. Light only leaks from heaven during Angelic visitations, which are typically accompanied by dangerous earthquakes, lightning strikes, tornados, and the like. Neil's strategy is like solving a maze by snaring an airplane passing overhead and being lifted over the maze's walls and directly to the exit. Neil knows that he is more likely to die in this endeavor than to succeed at his quest for exposure to heaven's light. But he chooses this strategy anyway. Against the odds, Neil

---

[8] The Biblical story of Job provides an example of someone whose faith and love of God does not waver, despite the tremendous undeserved ills that befall him.

succeeds in achieving exposure to heaven's light and becoming unconditionally committed to God. But in the final ironic twist, he is sent to hell anyway.[9]

Hell Is the Absence of God ends with Neil roaming Hell. Because he has been exposed to Heaven's light, he loves God unconditionally. He does not resent God for undeservedly sending him to Hell. He continues to love God despite all the evidence he has for the almighty's poor and nonsensical behavior. A similar response is available to anyone faced with the problem of making sense of God's actions. But here Chiang's *reductio* comes on strong. Neil is no longer a creature of reason who thinks freely. He is certainly not someone a philosopher, or any individual who values free thought or the power of reason, should seek to emulate. Neil is more like someone who has fallen under a spell and lost the power to think for themself. If the target of Neil's love (God) were revealed tomorrow to be a serial-killing rapist or a manifestation of the devil in disguise all along, Neil would still love God, and unconditionally. Neil might even say, "The Lord works in mysterious ways". But, at this point, Neil is a character to be pitied, and perhaps reviled, not emulated.

REFERENCES

Chiang, Ted. 2002. Hell Is The Absence of God. In *Stories of Your Life and Others*. Ted Chiang, 205–235. First Published in *Starlight 3*, 2001.
Hume, David. 1779. *Dialogues Concerning Natural Religion*.
Mackie, J. L. 1955. Evil and Omnipotence. *Mind* 64 (254): 200–212.
Plantinga, Alvin. 1974. *God, Freedom, and Evil*. New York: Harper and Row.
Rettler, Bradley. 2025. The Presence of Evil and the Absence of God. ???–??? of this volume.

---

[9] Here we get even more hard to explain behavior by God. If God can send the serial killer to heaven upon exposure to heaven's light, why can't God send Neil? Neil wasn't particularly devout or righteous before his death. But he didn't kill or rape anyone, and he demonstrated both great courage and love for his wife in the events leading up to his death.

PART III

Technology

CHAPTER 6

The Value of Fact and Feeling

Daniel Pallies

There are two stories within "The Truth of Fact, the Truth of Feeling." The first is the story of a journalist and father who writes a piece on *Remem*: a new technology that promises to replace one's natural memory by providing easy access to accurate recordings of one's life. The second story is about Jijingi, a young Tiv man who learns to read and write from a European missionary. Through their uses of technology—*Remem* and writing—both protagonists uncover facts that are inconsistent with what they feel to be true about their own lives. The unnamed journalist felt that he had overcome his selfishness to become a good father to his daughter, and Jijingi felt that his elders were on the right side of their arguments with other clans. But the journalist discovers that he was a much worse father than he had realized, and Jijingi discovers that his elders are in the wrong.

One of the questions these stories raise is what it takes to lead a good life. In particular, when the facts about our lives conflict with what we feel to be true about our lives, do the facts make any difference to how well our lives go for us? Or do only our feelings matter?

Philosophers have had much to say about this question. And many have argued that facts do matter; facts you don't know about can make your life

D. Pallies (✉)
Lingnan University, Tuen Mun, Hong Kong

© The Author(s), under exclusive license to Springer Nature Switzerland AG 2025
D. Friedell (ed.), *The Philosophy of Ted Chiang*,
https://doi.org/10.1007/978-3-031-81662-8_6

worse for you. But if this is correct, then each of us faces a problem. As the stories of the journalist and Jijingi illustrate, we might be ignorant of troubling facts about our lives, the sorts of facts that make our lives go worse for us. But if we are ignorant of these facts, then how can we possibly do anything about them? We all want to lead good lives, so if there is something that makes our lives worse for us—like the journalist's broken relationship with his daughter—it makes sense for us to try to fix it. But if we don't know what the relevant facts are, then what can we possibly do about them?

The Truth of Fact, the Truth of Feeling illustrates the scope of the practical problem we all face. But it also suggests a solution—actually two solutions. Not only do their stories illuminate an important practical problem, but they also show how this problem might be overcome.

6.1 Well-Being and Self-Deception

Philosophers use "well-being" or "welfare" to talk about how well someone's life is going for them. Having high well-being or high welfare means that your life is going well for you. It is hard to give a more exact definition than this, but not so hard to grasp the basic idea. When you are acting out of self-interest, you are trying to increase your well-being or make your life go better for you. And when you are acting in someone else's interests, you are trying to increase their well-being or make their life go better for them.

Thinking about well-being is an important part of morality. When Jijingi defers to the judgment of his elders, he does this because "it was their responsibility to decide what was best for the Shangev clan." This is naturally read as a thought about well-being: it is the responsibility of the elders to promote the well-being of the Shangev people, to ensure their lives go well. Similarly, when the journalist discovers the truth about his own parenting, he tells his daughter: "You deserve better." This isn't merely an acknowledgment that he failed in his obligations toward her. It's a recognition of how that failing affected her and made her worse off than she deserved.

There are lots of questions we can ask about well-being. But the important question, for present purposes, is whether facts you don't know can raise or lower your well-being. Was the journalist worse off for having a strained relationship with his daughter, even before he knew this? Was

Jijingi worse off for trusting his elder's false claims, before he learned the facts?

In one sense, it is obvious that facts you don't know about can make a difference to your well-being. They can make you worse off by causing other things that make you worse off. Suppose that an arsonist lights your home on fire while you are in it. Even if you never know that you are a victim of arson, it made you worse off—because the arson caused the fire, and the fire made you worse off.

The more interesting question is whether an unknown fact can make you worse off, not by virtue of having bad effects but directly. The philosopher Shelly Kagan illustrates the question:

> Imagine a man who dies contented, thinking he has achieved everything he wanted in life: his wife and family love him, he is a respected member of the community, and he has founded a successful business. Or so he thinks. In reality, however, he has been completely deceived: his wife cheated on him, his daughter and son were only nice to him so that they would be able to borrow the car, the other members of the community only pretended to respect him for the sake of the charitable contributions he sometimes made, and his business partner has been embezzling funds from the company which will soon go bankrupt. (Kagan 1994, 311)

None of this has any bad effects on the businessman, because he "dies contented." But even so, Kagan tells us, "it is difficult to believe that it is all a life could be, that this life has gone about as well as a life could go" (Kagan 1994, 311). And many people agree. A popular (though not universal)[1] reaction is that the businessman's life would have been better if his family really did love him, if he really was well-respected in the community, and if his business really were successful. The man dies believing that his life has been wonderful, but the facts don't support that belief.

It's easy to suppose that this philosophical point is irrelevant to our actual lives. The businessman in Kagan's story remains ignorant of important facts about his life because those facts are deliberately hidden from him. And the people doing the hiding are not just a few shady characters, but everyone in his life. He is, as Kagan says, "completely deceived." It's

---

[1] According to the view called "experientialism," only experiences make us better- or worse-off. Experientialists will say that because the businessman had all the experiences of a wonderful life, his life really was wonderful. Experientialism is a minority position in philosophy, but a substantial minority.

probably a safe assumption that you are not completely deceived like this. And you might think that, so long as you are not completely deceived by everyone in your life, you will not remain ignorant of important facts about your life. So it is possible for you to be worse off than you think, but in practical terms it is very unlikely.

It is exactly this sort of complacent attitude that is challenged by Chiang's story of the unnamed journalist. The journalist was not at the center of any community-wide conspiracy. We get no indication that his daughter ever lied to him about their relationship. But still, he was deceived—not by some other member of his family or community but by himself. He enjoins the reader directly:

> You may say, "I know I'm not perfect. I've made mistakes." I am here to tell you that you have made more than you think, that some of the core assumptions on which your self-image is built are actually lies.

Of course, this is a fictional character talking, and his claims are backed by fictional, memory-enhancing technology. Still, there are good reasons to take these claims seriously.

For one thing, there is ample psychological evidence that our memories are biased in our own favor. We tend to remember events that enhance our self-esteem and forget events that undermine it. We tend to take credit for our past successes, but describe our failures as the result of outside influences. We think about our failures less often than our successes, and when we do reflect on our failures, we tend to focus on how we have overcome those failures to become better people.[2] This empirical evidence gives us good reason to think that you and I, like Kagan's deceived businessman, could be ignorant of important facts about our lives. We all want to forget some of what we have done and some of what has happened to us, and we are very good at forgetting and misremembering.

Still, you might ask, how is this relevant to how well our lives are going for us now? The past is past. Even if you have badly deceived yourself about some of what has happened in your life, why would that mean that you are wrong about how well your life is going in the present?

---

[2] These claims receive support from a number of studies in the psychology of memory. For a sample of particularly relevant studies, see Alicke and Sedikides (2011); Ritchie et al. (2017); Alicke and Sedikides (2011); Walker et al. (2003); and Wilson and Ross (2001).

The answer is that, as the journalist says, "People are made of stories." When you think about how your life is going, this is at least partly a matter of thinking about the narrative arc of your life, not just a snapshot of your present. And if you are mistaken about your own past, then you can also be mistaken about the stories that are true of you now.

Perhaps some of your relationships with friends or family are not as strong as you think. Perhaps your accomplishments are not as great as you believe, or you are giving yourself too much credit for them. And perhaps you simply aren't the person you think you are—you are more prone to prejudice, cowardice, or selfishness than you realize. "Because all of us have been wrong on various occasions, engaged in cruelty and hypocrisy," the journalist tells us, "and we've forgotten most of those occasions." If you can be badly mistaken about all this—and you probably are at least somewhat mistaken—then you might end up being badly mistaken about how well your life is going for you. Some facts about your life are unknown to you, and these facts make you worse off.

Ordinarily, if something is making us worse off, then we want to do something about it. But what can we do when the facts that make us worse off are also unknown to us? What could the journalist have done, for example, if he never discovered the truth about his relationship with his daughter? He would never have known that there was any damage to repair. He would have spent his whole life thinking that his relationship with his daughter, and by extension, his own life, were better than they really were. If we can avoid this situation for ourselves, we should at least try. But how?

6.2 What Can We Do?

The stories of the journalist and Jijingi provide a few potential solutions. The most dramatic is to use *Remem*, but this is not an option for us (yet). Other solutions have less to do with technology and more to do with the way that we think about our own lives. At the end of their stories, the journalist and Jijingi make a choice about how to think about their lives, and both of their choices at least partly ameliorate the practical problem.

The journalist realizes that he does not know himself as well as he thought. Even before he learned about the facts about his blowout fight with his daughter, he recognized (and celebrated!) the fact that organic memory is imperfect. But after learning the facts, he realizes just how badly he knows himself. He asks: "How much personal insight can I claim if I can't trust my memory?" And this humility, this recognition that he does not know himself, is itself a partial solution to the practical problem.

To see how the journalist's humility provides a partial solution, we need to think about what sorts of facts might make us worse off. I mentioned a few examples: the facts of your relationships, accomplishments, and personality might be different than you think, in ways that you would find disturbing if only you knew. But another example is the *very fact that* you are mistaken about your relationships, accomplishments, or personality. Most of us would be distressed to discover that we are badly mistaken about our own lives. When the journalist discovers the facts about his relationship with his daughter, he is disturbed by the reality of their relationship but also by the fact that he was so badly mistaken about it.

If we embrace a kind of radical humility about our self-knowledge, then we avoid making this kind of mistake. To the extent that we are less confident in our beliefs about our lives, we are less badly mistaken if those beliefs turn out to be false. And if we become less badly mistaken about our own lives, this would be a way in which our lives take a turn for the better. So we can become better off by simply becoming less confident in the stories we tell ourselves about our own lives—by admitting, with the journalist, that we do not really know ourselves.

Jijingi's response suggests a very different solution to our practical problem. Jijingi chooses to ignore the documented facts about his clan's ancestry, in favor of what his elders say. He decides he cares more about what is best for the community, as opposed to the exact points of fact.

How could this provide even a partial solution to the practical problem? If certain facts can make us worse off without us knowing about them, then how can it help us to willfully disregard those facts? The answer lies in finding an explanation for why certain facts can make us worse off, despite being unknown to us. Why is the journalist worse off as a result of having a strained relationship with his daughter? Perhaps because he cares about it; he cares whether he has a strained relationship with his daughter. If this is right, then whether we care about some fact can make a difference to whether that fact makes us worse off. And it starts to make sense how Jijingi is responding effectively to the practical problem.

Jijingi chooses to stop caring about what the European documents say about his clan's history. He chooses to be more concerned with the decisions of his elders, not because they reflect the historical facts but because they are guiding the clan forward. If what we care about can make a difference to which facts make us worse off, then Jijingi's decisions might change his well-being. Going forward, the decisions of his elders might continue to contradict the historical facts. But if Jijingi does not care about those facts, then they may have no significance for his well-being.

Where does this leave us? Each of us cares about certain things in our lives: we tell ourselves stories about our relationships, our personal histories, our achievements, our growth as people. But the stories we tell ourselves may be contradicted by the facts, and our lives are worse for it. To that extent we are like Kagan's businessman, though we are deceived by ourselves rather than by deceitful friends and family. I do not know how exactly we should respond to this practical problem. Should we follow the journalist and forswear the stories we tell ourselves about our lives, or should we follow Jijingi and stop caring about whether those stories are factual? Neither option would be easy. But if we do nothing to respond to the practical problem, then we are likely worse off than we realize.

References

Alicke, Mark D., and Constantine Sedikides. 2011. *Handbook of Self-Enhancement and Self-Protection.* New York: Guilford Press.

Kagan, Shelly. 1994. Me and My Life. *Proceedings of the Aristotelian Society* 94:309–324. https://doi.org/10.1093/aristotelian/94.1.309.

Ritchie, Timothy D., Constantine Sedikides, and John J. Skowronski. 2017. Does a Person Selectively Recall the Good or the Bad from Their Personal Past? It Depends on the Recall Target and the Person's Favourability of Self-Views. *Memory (Hove, London)* 25 (8): 934–944. https://doi.org/10.1080/09658211.2016.1233984.

Walker, W. Richard, John J. Skowronski, and Charles P. Thompson. 2003. Life Is Pleasant–and Memory Helps to Keep It That Way. *Review of General Psychology* 7 (2): 203–210. https://doi.org/10.1037/1089-2680.7.2.203.

Wilson, Anne E., and Michael Ross. 2001. From Chump to Champ: People's Appraisals of Their Earlier and Present Selves. *Journal of Personality and Social Psychology* 80 (4): 572–584. https://doi.org/10.1037/0022-3514.80.4.572.

CHAPTER 7

We Can Remember It for You Better: Ted Chiang on Technology and Human Knowledge

Don Fallis

7.1 Introduction

Science fiction asks the question, "What If?" What if we could travel to other planets? What if we were to contact alien beings? What if we could visit the past? Ted Chiang's work is certainly in this vein. He often asks, what if we had a brand new technology? How would this technology affect how we experience the world? In particular, how might this technology impact how and what we *know* about the world?

In several stories, such as "Anxiety Is the Dizziness of Freedom," "The Lifecycle of Software Objects," "The Merchant and the Alchemist's Gate," "Story of Your Life," and "What's Expected of Us," Chiang considers how technology can transform human cognition and knowledge. The

---

D. Fallis (✉)
Boston, MA, USA
e-mail: d.fallis@northeastern.edu

© The Author(s), under exclusive license to Springer Nature Switzerland AG 2025
D. Friedell (ed.), *The Philosophy of Ted Chiang*,
https://doi.org/10.1007/978-3-031-81662-8_7

novelette "The Truth of Fact, the Truth of Feeling" is his most careful evaluation of the knowledge-related pros and cons of a new technology.[1]

In the near future, people wear "personal cams that capture continuous video of their entire lives." And by allowing quick search and retrieval from these "lifelogs," a new technology called "Remem" enables us to "remember" almost all of our experiences with perfect fidelity. Thereby, it significantly improves our knowledge of our own past. However, the narrator of Chiang's novelette, a journalist writing about this technology, is skeptical about such enhancement of our organic memory. For instance, he thinks that it is important to allow bad memories to fade over time and for us to embellish good memories. But after trying Remem for himself, the journalist discovers important benefits of the technology, such as it not being quite so easy to deceive ourselves.

The idea of a device that records everything we see and can play it back for us (or someone else) is not new to science fiction. It appears in John Crowley's classic short story "Snow" and in the *Black Mirror* episode "The Entire History of You." But Chiang offers a more nuanced evaluation of its effect on human cognition and knowledge. Given that we may have this sort of technology in the fairly near future, this is an urgent and important task to get right.

In this chapter, I discuss how philosophers have recently engaged in the same sort of evaluative project with respect to many other technologies, such as smartphones, social media, and the internet. They have raised concerns about these technologies that are very similar to Chiang's concerns about Remem. I disagree with these pessimistic assessments and argue that, on balance, these technologies, including Remem, are likely to be beneficial.

7.2 Epistemic Evaluations

Chiang's work can be seen as contributing to the area of philosophy known as *applied epistemology*. *Epistemology* is the study of what knowledge is and how people can acquire it. *Applied* epistemology focuses specifically on real-life issues that people confront when seeking knowledge. In other words, applied epistemology bears the same relation to epistemology that the better-known field of applied ethics bears to ethics.

---

[1] Chiang has also written non-fiction in this vein. See, for example, his recent piece in the *New Yorker* on "ChatGPT is a Blurry JPEG of the Web."

Philosophers working in applied epistemology have given *epistemic evaluations* of several new technologies. In the early days of the internet, Paul Thagard (1997) analyzed how it can help scientists to acquire knowledge. When Wikipedia first appeared and people worried about the reliability of an encyclopedia that anyone can edit, I evaluated this particular website (Fallis 2011). More recently, Michael Lynch (2016) comprehensively evaluated the internet as a source of knowledge.

Moreover, much like Chiang, philosophers have even studied the knowledge-related pros and cons of technologies that do not yet exist. We can currently access the internet at any time or place with smartphones. But Lynch considers an even more immediate brain-internet connection that he calls *neuromedia*. This sort of technology appears in science fiction (as in Iain M. Banks's Culture novels) and Elon Musk's Neuralink Corporation is currently trying to implement it.

These evaluations typically compare a technology, along several knowledge-related dimensions, to alternative sources for the same sort of information. For example, I compared Wikipedia to traditional encyclopedias using a framework developed by Alvin Goldman (1987). We can evaluate Remem in the same way.

According to Goldman, the knowledge-related dimensions that we should consider are:

Power—how many different true beliefs can people acquire by using the technology?
Speed—how fast can people acquire these true beliefs?
Fecundity—how many people can acquire true beliefs by using the technology?
Reliability—how many true beliefs do people acquire relative to the number of false beliefs that they acquire?

Remem does very well compared to organic memory on these dimensions. First, it is certainly more powerful than organic memory. That is, we can access much more information than we could naturally. Most notably, we would never forget anything that ever happened to us. In addition, we could even retrieve details that we did not notice originally.

Second, Remem is just as speedy as organic memory. Indeed, this is the big selling point for Remem. According to the story, there were lifelogs before Remem. But except in special circumstances, it was prohibitively time-consuming to search through them.

Third, Remem seems to be more fecund than organic memory. Of course, we have always been able to share our memories with other people by talking to them. But with Remem, we can literally share our memories. For example, to try out Remem, the journalist does not use his own lifelog. He had not been recording one. Instead, he cobbles a lifelog together from the lifelogs of people he has interacted with.

Finally, and most importantly, Remem is more reliable than organic memory. Indeed, the turning point of the story is when we learn that the journalist's organic memory is not trustworthy. Regarding a fight with his daughter after his wife left him, he had "fabricated a narrative that bore little resemblance to reality" because he could not accept that he was "the kind of father who could say such a thing to his child." Remem reveals the truth to the journalist and to us.

Existing technologies that supplement our memory already provide these sorts of knowledge-related benefits. As Clive Thompson (2007) claims, "the perfect recall of silicon memory can be an enormous boon to thinking." For example, when I first saw the aforementioned *Black Mirror* episode, I couldn't remember where I had seen the actor who played the wife before. I had to look her up on the Internet Movie Database (IMDb) to recall that she had played one of the main characters in the mystery series, *Broadchurch*. And even if I could have dredged up where I'd seen this actor before, it still would have been faster to just look her up on IMDb.

As noted above, people worry about the reliability of crowdsourced databases like IMDb and Wikipedia. These databases contain inaccurate information since they are compiled by humans and humans make mistakes. But as James Surowiecki (2004) notes, a large enough group can be more reliable than a single expert. And it can certainly be better than my own unaided memory. In any event, this worry doesn't arise with Remem. The personal cams record what happens without human interference.

Moreover, we have seen these advantages over organic memory with an even older technology, writing. As Chiang points out, "we don't normally think of it as such, but writing is a technology, which means that a literate person is someone whose thought processes are technologically mediated." In addition to evaluating Remem in his novelette, Chiang evaluates writing. Interspersed with the journalist's story, he tells the story of a boy named Jijingi from the preliterate culture of Tivland. When exposed to writing by a European missionary, Jijingi learns of the many knowledge-related benefits of this technology. But like the journalist, he eventually sees that the costs can also be great.

7.3 Breakdowns and Interference

Of course, a technology is only powerful, speedy, fecund, and reliable if we can access it. Admittedly, people sometimes lose access to their organic memories. In addition to more mundane examples of forgetting, people get blackout drunk, have strokes, and might even have an iron rod driven into their skulls (a la Phineas Gage). But technology can be subject to catastrophic failure. And when it fails, we may not just lose the extra benefits that the technology provides. We may end up worse off than we were before we had the technology.

When a technology like Remem or neuromedia is so tightly integrated with our organic systems, it can radically affect how those systems operate. In particular, we might rely so much on the technology that we become unable to perform certain cognitive tasks without it. For example, according to Lynch, "an over dependence on neuromedia might atrophy the ability to access information in other ways." Thus, "losing neuromedia is an immensely unsettling experience; it's like a normally sighted person going blind." Moreover, the ability to carry out certain cognitive tasks on our own might never develop in the first place. Indeed, in Chiang's novelette, because the journalist's daughter grew up with assistive technology, "she can speak fluently but can only barely write."

So, if Remem were to breakdown, even temporarily, we would essentially lose our memory. As Chiang points out, echoing Lynch, "an obvious drawback to such reliance is the possibility that people might become virtual amnesiacs whenever the software crashes." Indeed, this happens to some degree with existing technologies that supplement our memory. As Thompson observes, we don't remember phone numbers anymore since we rely on our smartphone to remember them for us.[2]

---

[2] Even writing might put our memory at risk in this way. In the *Phaedrus*, Plato warned that the art of writing "will create forgetfulness in the learners' souls, because they will not use their memories; they will trust to the external written characters and not remember of themselves."

However, the risk of breakdown should not deter us from adopting these technologies. After all, we rely on all sorts of technologies (automobiles, electricity grids, computers, etc.) that break down occasionally. But the benefits are sufficiently large that we put up with the occasional inconvenience of a breakdown. As Lynch nicely puts it, "when the zombie apocalypse comes, you want to be able to stand on your own. But this isn't the zombie apocalypse."

Of course, a technology that connects the brain to external devices is not just susceptible to accidental breakdowns. It is also susceptible to interference by adversaries. By erasing information, adversaries reduce the technology's power. Changing information reduces its reliability. Even simply observing information might indirectly reduce its power and reliability. For instance, such surveillance can have a chilling effect on our willingness to seek out controversial information and experiences. Moreover, the data gathered by such surveillance can be used to target us with misleading online content.

The written word is subject to such adversarial interference. For example, as the chief of Jijingi's clan points out, the scribes from the mission school "wield their knowledge of writing like a long gun; they demand their chiefs find them wives, or else they'll write lies about them and have the Europeans depose them." Similarly, even more sophisticated technologies like Remem can be hacked. When the journalist uses Remem to recall the fight with his daughter, his "first thought was that it must be a fake, that Nicole had edited the video to put her words into my mouth." Indeed, some videos in people's lifelogs could be deepfakes. The journalist only accepts the truth after he had "asked Remem to examine the video's watermark, and it reported the video was unmodified."

Adversaries can implant fake memories into organic memory. It does not require the sophisticated technology of Philip K. Dick's "We Can Remember It for You Wholesale." For example, the psychologist Elizabeth Loftus (1995) famously convinced subjects that they had been lost in a mall as children. But it is certainly possible to interfere with memories if they are stored on external devices as lifelogs presumably are.

Even so, the risk of interference should not deter us from adopting such technologies. They are still likely to be more powerful and reliable than our organic memories. After all, even if adversaries are less able to mess with our organic memories, we are, as Chiang's novelette highlights, pretty good at unconsciously messing with them all by ourselves.

7.4 Facts Without Understanding

Let's set aside concerns about breakdowns and interference. Chiang's *main* worry is about what happens when Remem works just as it is intended to. As the journalist says, "just as worrying to me as the prospect of technological failure was that of technological success."

Successful technologies can change *how* we think. For example, in "Story of Your Life," when a linguist learns the graphical writing system of an alien species, it profoundly changes how she experiences the world. She can essentially see into the future. And in "The Truth of Fact, the Truth of Feeling," Chiang asks us to "imagine what will happen if children begin using Remem to access those lifelogs: their mode of cognition will diverge from ours because the act of recall will be different."

Chiang worries that we will lose something with Remem rather than gain something. For example, he points out that if we only see our "past through the unblinking eye of a video camera," we will be unable to "soften harsh memories" or to "romanticiz[e] childhood memories."

Chiang may be correct that erasing bad memories and embellishing good memories are useful skills. After all, our memories play important roles in our lives beyond just providing factual information about our past. But if we modify some of our memories, don't we end up *knowing* less about our past than we did before?

Admittedly, there probably is knowledge that it is better not to have. Indeed, this is a fairly common trope in science fiction. For example, H. P. Lovecraft warns in "The Case of Charles Dexter Ward" that there are "things no mortal ought ever to know." But these are cases where practical considerations outweigh knowledge-related considerations. Thus, this takes us beyond the scope of a purely *epistemic* evaluation.

However, the very title of the novelette suggests that Chiang has a concern about Remem that should be part of a knowledge-related evaluation. Remem gives us better access to "truth of fact." But it does not give us access to "truth of feeling." According to the journalist, "continuous video of my entire childhood would be full of facts but devoid of feeling, simply because cameras couldn't capture the emotional dimension of events."

Philosophers have raised similar concerns about the internet. It gives us a faster and more reliable way to access *factual* information. But as a result, the internet can divert us from other more important knowledge-related endeavors. For example, Nicholas Carr (2008) argues that the internet causes us to lose our ability and desire to concentrate on longer and more complicated texts. Also, Lynch argues that the internet causes us to more readily accept what we read without due reflection.

Much like Carr and Lynch, Chiang has a legitimate knowledge-related concern about Remem. Easier access to truth of fact can diminish our access to truth of feeling. Similarly, Lynch claims that "our digital form of life, while giving us more facts, is not particularly good at giving us more understanding." However, before we decide against adopting a technology, we should **(a)** explore the full range of its potential benefits and **(b)** consider the possibilities for mitigating its downsides. As I argue below, the potential knowledge-related benefits of Remem go beyond replacing and improving organic memory. In addition, the technology might be enhanced to provide greater access to truth of feeling.

Modern society was largely created by information processing technologies such as the written word, the printing press, and the internet. These technologies are not just supplements to memory. They allow us to more easily share information. (Remember that Remem enhances fecundity as well as power and reliability.) The resulting collaborations have led to knowledge that has transformed the world.

Remem could be the next step in this evolution. What if we could share memories as easily as we now share documents? In addition, scientists and corporations make valuable discoveries by collecting huge amounts of data and using sophisticated algorithms to search for patterns. What if we could apply big data analysis to our memories? The technology has important applications beyond married couples (such as the one interviewed by the journalist) "settl[ing] arguments over who had actually said what, using the video record to prove they were right."

Of course, as we have discussed, there are also knowledge-related downsides to Remem. Just as the internet insufficiently promotes reflective knowledge and understanding, Remem insufficiently promotes knowledge of truth of feeling. But there may be further technological advances that get this right. Remem does not record what our past experiences felt like. But we can easily imagine technologies that facilitate this sort of recollection. Indeed, even before the written word, the printing press, and the internet, we used external aids to memory, from *memory theatres* to scrapbooks, that brought back feelings as well as facts.

Acknowledgments For extremely helpful feedback, I would like to thank David Friedell, Kay Mathiesen, Dan Zelinski, and the participants in the Ted Chiang and Philosophy workshop at Union College.

References

Carr, Nicholas. 2008. Is Google Making Us Stupid?: What the Internet Is Doing to Our Brains. *The Atlantic.* https://www.theatlantic.com/magazine/archive/2008/07/is-google-making-us-stupid/306868/

Fallis, Don. 2011. Wikipistemology. In *Social Epistemology: Essential Readings*, ed. Alvin Goldman and Dennis Whitcomb, 297–313. Oxford: Oxford University Press.

Goldman, Alvin I. 1987. Foundations of Social Epistemics. *Synthese* 73:109–144.

Loftus, Elizabeth F., and Jacqueline E. Pickrell. 1995. The Formation of False Memories. *Psychiatric Annals* 25:720–725.

Lynch, Michael P. 2016. *The Internet of Us: Knowing More and Understanding Less in the Age of Big Data*. New York: W. W. Norton.

Surowiecki, James. 2004. *The Wisdom of Crowds*. New York: Doubleday.

Thagard, Paul. 1997. Internet Epistemology: Contributions of New Information Technologies to Scientific Research. http://cogsci.uwaterloo.ca/Articles/Pages/Epistemology.html

Thompson, Clive. 2007. Your Outboard Brain Knows All. *Wired..* https://www.wired.com/2007/09/st-thompson-3/.

PART IV

Existentialism

CHAPTER 8

How to Live With Freedom

Katherine Ward

My three-year-old son loves jump-scares. When I jump out from behind a door or piece of furniture, he screams and laughs and within seconds he'll point to where I was hiding and say, "Surprise me again!" I try to explain that it doesn't work if he's expecting it. Surprises work only when you don't know you're about to be surprised.

Surprise isn't the only experience like this—many experiences seem to require that something about the experience remains hidden. Try to think about how you move your fingers as you type, the way your eyes travel across the page as you read. You will no longer be immersed in what you are doing; you will stumble through. Your activity is interrupted by making explicit to yourself, by revealing, some part of the activity. Aspects of an experience must sometimes be forgotten for the experience itself to emerge.

Much of what is written on existential freedom suggests that *it* may be one of these "hidden" experiences. On an existential understanding, freedom is our ability to care about who we are and to make choices about who we want to be in the future. We can step back from the way the world actually is and imagine how it ought to be, reflect on *who* we ought to be, and to call into question, reject, or recommit ourselves to our most basic values. This view of freedom means we are responsible for what we *do* value and commit ourselves to. As I decline another game of "surprise" to go work, I am choosing not just one project over another, but what I value. I invest my time and energy here and not there. I am choosing who I am—the kind of mother I am, the kind of scholar I am.

Accepting our freedom can be deeply unsettling. As Sartre points out people often "flee" from their freedom, acting in bad faith by pretending their actions and choices are handed down—dictated by the roles they occupy, the life they have led, fate, or causal determinism. Heidegger suggests that even if we don't flee from recognizing our freedom, we often simply "fall" into our activities. We disperse our attention and awareness into our projects, letting them take us over, and so "forget" about the connection between what we are doing and who we are. We may forget our freedom for good reason. The direct experience of freedom in *anxiety* is an overwhelming and disturbing experience that utterly stops one from participating in life. But even just thinking explicitly about the fact that I am choosing my values and who I am every time I leave for work, decide on lunch, pick out a movie, would be an interruption—like thinking about my fingers as I type. Living authentically, however, requires recognizing our freedom and making choices in light of this understanding. Authenticity demands facing our freedom and responsibility. How can one live authentically if we must forget our freedom to enact it?

Many of Ted Chiang's stories explore the idea that there are some truths that, if confronted and believed, threaten commitments and activities that keep us anchored in human life. In this chapter, I'll draw on Chiang's stories to explore existential freedom, anxiety, and authenticity and offer one possible way of understanding how one can live authentically in everyday life.

8.1 Freedom

We often think of freedom or "free will" as the ability to choose between two or more options. I choose to eat a sandwich instead of a salad; I choose to stop and help someone who looks lost as opposed to walking by. What makes the choice *free*, some argue, is that I might have done something else. I *did* help the lost tourist, but I could have chosen not to. Many philosophers think this ability to "do otherwise" is a requirement for free will and for morality. However, the existential concept of freedom is different from an ability to do otherwise. Existential freedom emphasizes *how* we reason and make choices, and how our choices are tied to caring about who we are and ought to be.

As a teenager I remember being horrified by the prospect of being seen shopping at Walmart. My (definitely classist) fear was rooted in the fact that I didn't want to be the kind of person who shopped at Walmart. Now when I go into Walmart I feel guilty—it's convenient but threatens small businesses and is brutal in its price suppression tactics. I don't want to be the kind of person who supports those practices. The *way* I shop also draws on my desire to be a certain kind of person. I smile all the time, always make sure to tell the cashiers to have a good day. I want to be the kind of person who is polite to others and recognizes their humanity in, at least, a small way. There is this special human style of moving about the world. Our choices and actions are bound up with worries and hopes about who we are. We are able, as Sartre says, "to leave the level of being in order frankly to approach that of non-being"—the world of possibility (Sartre 1956, 434). I can step back from what I am doing to consider if I *ought* to do it. I can think about what this or that activity or project says about the kind of person I am and if I like that person or want to be a different kind of person. Similarly, reflecting on one's past means navigating a minefield of shame, pride, regret—all of which inform your understanding of who you are now and what you ought to do going forward. This ability to care and plan and act is freedom, and it is inescapable—whether I could actually do otherwise or not, feeling responsible for my choice is required for the caring that is at the heart of our human style of being in the world. If you *really* did not feel responsible, you could not care or invest the kind of thought and concern that allows you to choose in the special human way that is free.

Chiang's stories "What's Expected of Us" and "Story of Your Life" help illustrate existential freedom. In "What's Expected of Us," a small device called a Predictor proves that we cannot "do otherwise." The device has only a button and a small green light, which flashes exactly one second before the button is pushed. It works through a negative time delay, so it is impossible to "trick" the Predictor. If you see the light flash, the button is inevitably pressed. If you wait for the light with the intention of *not* pressing the button, it never lights. If you think the ability to do otherwise is essential for free will, this is a fatalistic threat to free will, and, in the story, many people who play with the Predictor simply stop willing anything at all. "Like a legion of Bartleby the scriveners, they no longer engage in spontaneous action" (Chiang 2019, 59). They cease to act, feed themselves, talk, etc. An existential philosopher, however, would be unmoved by the Predictor or see the set nature of future action as a threat to freedom. If the light blinks when I resolve not to press the button or doesn't blink when I do, that only means that something happens between the moment of my initial decision and the future that changes my resolve or that interrupts my plan. It does not mean that I ceased thinking, deliberating, making choices or caring about them. It does not mean I'm not *free*.

In contrast to those who succumb to the Predictor, Louise Banks in "Story of Your Life" embraces her freedom in the face of a set and static future. Louise becomes fluent in an extraterrestrial language with the unexpected result that her consciousness becomes unbound from a sequential experience of time. She can "remember" the future and the past as she experiences the present. She thus comes to know her future. She knows, before her daughter is born, how her daughter will die and that she will die young. Louise doesn't try to stop the unfolding of events, but not because she has surrendered her control or her responsibility. She is no mere passenger in her story. Louise understands the inevitability of her future actions, but in a way that is consistent with her owning them. As she "spontaneously" buys a bowl on a shopping trip—an action she knows she will do—she muses:

> I reached out and took the bowl from the shelf. The motion didn't feel like something I was forced to do. Instead it seemed just as urgent as my rushing to catch the bowl when it falls on you: an instinct that I felt right in following.
> 'I could use a salad bowl like this.' (Chiang 2016b, 133)

Louise has been transformed by knowing the future; her values and preferences are radically altered—but they are still her *own*. She now has a "sense of urgency, a sense of obligation to act precisely as she knew she would" (Chiang 2016b, 132). Louise still chooses her future; she still grapples with the choices she makes. She simply knows, wants, and chooses the future that is.

8.2 Anxiety and Authenticity

In existentialism, *authenticity* doesn't mean being true to some secret inner "you"; it doesn't mean living in a way that will necessarily make you happier or more fulfilled. Rather, authenticity means recognizing the kind of being you are. You are *free*—you care about who you are and this caring is the ground of all your choices and actions—and you are *responsible* for who you are—your actions shape who you are and what you can do in the future. To live authentically is to embrace freedom and responsibility in everyday life Existentialists talk about authenticity as something one ought to strive for; understanding the kind of creature we are should inform the way we live our lives. However, it is equally clear that the direct experience of freedom is unsustainable and incompatible with everyday life. Directly experiencing freedom is called, by various authors (and translators), "dread," "anxiety," or "angst"—in all cases, being directly acquainted with freedom is like dropping a bomb in your life.

Everyone has experienced anxiety about something—a test, a break-up, a job interview. Existential anxiety isn't *that*. Existential anxiety has no definite source; there is nothing I can point to and say *that* is making me anxious. Existential anxiety is general, "completely indefinite" (Heidegger 2008, 231). It's like a fog, and in this fog everything you normally find valuable and meaningful seems insignificant. Have you ever felt like you didn't recognize the world you lived in? Like you didn't know why you were doing what you were doing? What the point of any of your projects and goals were—the *real* point? You look around at all the stuff you've accumulated and thought ... but *why?* The totality of your "involvements" (the equipment, projects, usually cherished relationships) is suddenly "of no consequence; it collapses into itself; the world has the character of completely lacking significance" (Heidegger 2008, 231). We stop caring about all the things we normally *do* care about, and when this happens, we stop understanding who we are. I am a constellation of my roles and relationships—the mother of two children, a philosopher, cat-lover, ambivalent shopper at Walmart—and also the equipment and paraphernalia that allows me to stay in those roles—our two-hundred-year-old house, handed down furniture, my work clothes/parent clothes. All of these things I have chosen, expressed a commitment or value for, and in doing that, I have made myself who I am. When these fall away and shrink to "insignificance," I can't understand myself through them. Who am I if I'm not committed to any of these things? Anxiety, in this way, robs us of our ability to understand who we are (Heidegger 2008, 232).

The experience of anxiety directly acquaints us with our freedom, because in anxiety we withdraw our care from everything and in its absence, we do not know who we are. We, in fact, *cannot* know who we are because who we are just *is* our caring—our commitments to these projects, those relationships, and the equipment and paraphernalia that sustain them. What makes us anxious is the recognition that we are responsible for renewing our commitments and values, for investing our projects and lives with meaning, and that our lives have meaning only to the extent that we continue doing these things. What makes us anxious, as Heidegger sometimes puts it, is possibility. Things are the way they are and I am the way I am, because I have chosen it (Heidegger 2008, 232). To borrow a title from one of Chiang's works—"Anxiety is the Dizziness of Freedom."

Although living authentically cannot mean living in a permanent state of anxiety, it must require more than abstract acceptance of our freedom. It must be felt in a way that consistently shapes our actions. Chiang's stories "What's Expected of Us" and "Division By Zero" persuasively demonstrate why. In the former story, there are compelling arguments that free will is an illusion, but "no one ever really accepts the conclusion" (Chiang 2019, 59). The direct demonstration of the Predictor makes the truth felt and profoundly shapes the actions (or inactions) of many. Similarly, in "Division By Zero," the main character, Renee, proves that Arithmetic as a formal system is inconsistent—that any number equals any other number. Renee is completely undone by this revelation, in part because she understands it not abstractly by following the argument but directly: "in its own perverted way, it *felt right*. She understood it, knew why it was true, believed it" (Chiang 2016a, 83). Unlike many of her peers, she is directly acquainted with the contradiction in a way that she cannot "forget."

Authenticity must require an understanding of freedom that is more than abstract acceptance; it must be felt deeply and at every instance to shape our behavior. However, it must also stop short of anxiety, which, if sustained, would have an effect similar to the akinetic mutism of "What's Expected of Us."

8.3 Living Authentically Everyday

Although Heidegger clearly thinks we can live authentically,[1] he never explains how. The work of another existential phenomenologist, Merleau-Ponty, provides some guidance. He borrowed heavily from Gestalt psychology, emphasizing the way our experience is always an organization of foreground and background. The background, though often "unthought," shapes essentially our experience of the foreground. We are rarely, for example, explicitly cognizant of how we draw on lighting context (daylight, incandescent light, candlelight) in our interpretation of color. We see color directly and without deliberation. Yet, we always draw on our understanding of lighting context in our experience of color. A white wall in the early dawn hours will appear "in spontaneous vision as white," but if we take a picture of the wall absent any clue about the lighting, it is blue-gray (Merleau-Ponty 2013, 320). Grocery store butcher cases are lined with green lettuce to contrast with and make more vivid the red of the meat. People generally don't (and aren't supposed to) notice this, but it still effectively shapes what they see.

To live authentically, freedom must be like this—never the focus of our everyday activity, but the background from which we make our choices. In authenticity, we don't "forget" our freedom, but it slips from our notice—affecting us just as lighting affects what we see, shaping it essentially but quietly. In "Story of Your Life," Louise knows that her daughter will die in a climbing accident when she's twenty-five. Louise sometimes thinks explicitly about this, but more often it is simply the background against which she interprets things.

> When you're three and we're climbing a steep, spiral flight of stairs, I'll hold your hand extra tightly. You'll pull your hand away from me. "I can do it by myself," you'll insist, and then move away from me to prove it ... We'll repeat that scene countless times during your childhood. I can almost believe that, given your contrary nature, my attempts to protect you will be what create your love of climbing: first the jungle gym, at the playground, then trees out in the green belt around our neighborhood, the rock walls at the climbing club and ultimately cliff faces in national parks. (Chiang 2016b, 135)

---

[1] "[A]uthentic existence is not something which floats above falling everydayness; existentially, it is only a modified way in which such everydayness is seized upon" (Heidegger 2008, 224).

To live with your freedom is like this. Rarely, you experience the full force of freedom in anxiety. More often, you live with the background weight of it—shaping what you see and do. As I lay in bed reading to my son or talking to him about his day, I do sometimes balance between the current moment and vertigo of the future we are making. I know there will be a time when he wants to be with his friends and not me, when he will have his own family. I know it's possible we will have a falling out and won't talk, maybe won't love each other anymore. I feel how my own love for him can and will change even as I experience its absolute certainty now. I'm still "in the moment"—I'm not distracted from being with him. I'm being with him in a uniquely human way—thinking in the moment and beyond it—of what could be and what should be. I know that I am responsible both for the moment now and for who I become and we become in the future. It's both lovely and scary.

"Surprise me again!"

References

Chiang, Ted. 2016a. Division By Zero. In *Stories of Your Life and Others*, 71–89. New York: Vintage Books.

———. 2016b. Story of Your Life. In *Stories of Your Life and Others*, 91–145. New York: Vintage Books.

———. 2019. What's Expected of Us. In *Exhalation*, 58–61. New York: Alfred A. Knopf.

Heidegger, Martin. 2008. *Being and Time*. Trans. John Macquarrie and Edward Robinson. New York: Harper Perennial.

Merleau-Ponty, Maurice. 2013. *Phenomenology of Perception*. Trans. Donald Landes. New York: Routledge.

Sartre, Jean-Paul. 1956. *Being and Nothingness*. Trans. Hazel E. Barnes. New York: Philosophical Library.

CHAPTER 9

Existential Responsibility in Kierkegaard, Nietzsche, and Chiang

Justin White

9.1 Introduction

In "Story of Your Life" (2002) and "Anxiety Is the Dizziness of Freedom" (2019), Ted Chiang explores questions that would be at home in contemporary scholarship on free will, agency, and moral responsibility. In "Story of Your Life," Chiang asks whether knowledge of the future is compatible with free will. And the prism technology in "Anxiety Is the Dizziness of Freedom" prompts questions of whether we are responsible for out-of-character actions. If such actions were genuine anomalies, would we be less responsible for them? In these stories, however, these questions are entangled with questions more at home in the existentialist tradition. Put in conversation with Friedrich Nietzsche and Søren Kierkegaard, Chiang's stories present a compelling picture of existential responsibility and what it means to live a rich human existence, in particular, what it means to affirm our lives (Nietzsche) and to become selves (Kierkegaard).

On the face of it, Nietzsche's idea of eternal recurrence and Kierkegaard's notion of anxiety as the dizziness of freedom (*The Concept of Anxiety*)

J. White (✉)
Brigham Young University, Provo, UT, USA
e-mail: justin_white@byu.edu

push in very different directions.[1] Nietzsche asks how we would respond to learning that we would live our life over and over again to the exact detail; Kierkegaard highlights different responses to the dizzying array of possible life paths. Similarly, Chiang's "Story of Your Life" and "Anxiety Is the Dizziness of Freedom" push to opposite poles. One story asks how one could embrace a life if one knows one's future; the other asks how one could find one's choices meaningful if one could know that parallel versions of oneself can (and almost surely will!) choose differently. But despite these differences, Nietzsche, Kierkegaard, and Chiang all explore the question of how to take responsibility for oneself instead of succumbing to the temptation to offload responsibility for oneself and one's life.

9.2 Nietzsche's Eternal Recurrence, "Story of Your Life," and Choosing Your Life

As the range of chapters in this volume attests, "Story of Your Life" explores many philosophical questions, from the role of language in shaping experience (even reality) to the relationship between knowledge of the future and free will. The story initially suggests that free will is incompatible with knowledge of the future: "The existence of free will meant that we couldn't know the future" (132). However, the story soon complicates this picture, at least for the heptapods. "The heptapods," Louise writes, "are neither free nor bound as we understand those concepts ... within the context of simultaneous consciousness, freedom is not meaningful, but neither is coercion" (137). This is also the case, though to a lesser extent, for Louise as she learns Heptapod B and comes to inhabit a worldview that is "an amalgam of human and heptapod" (140).

However, even though the heptapods' language and simultaneous temporal consciousness put pressure on common ways of conceiving things, Louise goes on, "Freedom isn't an illusion; it's perfectly real in the context of sequential consciousness" (137). In that context, "knowledge of the future [is] incompatible with free will. What made it possible for me to exercise freedom of choice also made it impossible for me to know the future" (137). These questions about free will, in light of Louise's knowledge of Heptapod B, set the stage for Chiang's more Nietzschean

---

[1] Although the notion of eternal recurrence appears in other works, here I focus on its treatment in *The Gay Science*.

question: if Louise already knows her life's path, in what sense can she choose, even affirm, her life?

In *The Gay Science* 341, Nietzsche introduces the notion of eternal recurrence with the following passage:

> What, if some day or night a demon were to steal after you into your loneliest loneliness and say to you: "This life as you now live it and have lived it, you will have to live once more and innumerable times more; and there will be nothing new in it, but every pain and every joy and every thought and sigh and everything unutterably small or great in your life will have to return to you, all in the same succession and sequence—even this spider and this moonlight between the trees, and even this moment and I myself. The eternal hourglass of existence is turned upside down again and again, and you with it, speck of dust!"
>
> Would you not throw yourself down and gnash your teeth and curse the demon who spoke thus? Or have you once experienced a tremendous moment when you would have answered him: "You are a god and never have I heard anything more divine!" If this thought gained possession of you, it would change you as you are or perhaps crush you. The question in each and every thing, "Do you desire this once more and innumerable times more?" would lie upon your actions as the greatest weight. Or how well disposed would you have to become to yourself and to life to crave nothing more fervently than this ultimate eternal confirmation and seal? (Nietzsche 1974/1887)

The idea of eternal recurrence serves as a litmus test for how we are oriented toward our lives. If you were to receive this news, would you throw herself down and curse the demon? Or would you joyously receive it? Could the news that you would live your current life, in every detail, over and over again, be welcome?

Louise's situation is admittedly different. She knows the path of her life, but her life will not eternally recur. Moreover, while Louise knows her future, it is unclear whether the recipient of the demon's message would, in future existences, know the future or know that she had lived her life innumerable times before.

But both Nietzsche and Chiang press their readers to consider how they relate to their lives. How can we become so well-disposed to our lives that we can embrace it and joyously affirm it? As Louise muses, "From the beginning I knew my destination, and I chose my route accordingly. But am I working toward an extreme of joy, or of pain?" (145). "These questions are in my mind when your father asks me, 'Do you want to make a baby?' And I smile and answer, 'Yes,' and I unwrap his arms from around me, and we hold hands as we walk inside to make love, to make you" (145). Knowing her future—both joys and heartache—Louise chooses, even embraces, her path.

9.3 Becoming a Self: Self-Responsibility in Kierkegaard and Chiang

At first glance, Chiang's "Anxiety Is the Dizziness of Freedom" and Kierkegaard's *The Concept of* Anxiety present very different concerns from those explored in the previous section. Whereas eternal recurrence and "Story of Your Life" involve someone with only one path, Kierkegaard's conception of anxiety as "the dizziness of freedom" and Chiang's corresponding story involve an overwhelming abundance of possibilities. The question is less how to live your one life but how to respond to the dizzying array of possibilities that is the human condition. Both highlight the tendency to try to offload that responsibility as well as the difficulty of taking responsibility for your life.

Taking its title from *The Concept of Anxiety*, Chiang's story invokes quantum mechanics and parallel selves to explore topics ranging from regret and responsibility to the complexity of the self and the surprising consequences of minor events or actions. In *The Concept of Anxiety* Kierkegaard uses the biblical story of the fall to analyze human selfhood. As Kierkegaard describes it, a central feature of the story of Eden is anxiety. Anxiety, for Kierkegaard, is "the dizziness of freedom," the overwhelming and dizzying recognition that there are different ways to live and that we are responsible for how we live. Chiang's story illustrates various ways to avoid responsibility but also shows how we can become "selves" through what Kierkegaard calls a "qualitative leap," in which we take responsibility for our selves. Chiang's story also beautifully explores the balance between taking responsibility for our actions and not becoming paralyzed by this responsibility. Showing the dangers of both extremes, it suggests that getting it right often depends on others.

Claiming that "to become human does not come that easily,"[2] Kierkegaard consistently explores the idea of selfhood or individuality as an achievement, as well as different ways we can fall short. In *The Concept*

---

[2] Kierkegaard (1970), *Journals and Papers*, vol. 2, 278.

of Anxiety, he describes humans as a synthesis of the psychical and the physical, one which depends on a third unifying factor—spirit (43). Anxiety is not found in "the beast," because the beast is not "qualified as spirit," in the sense that the beast is not responsible for its behavior. Human beings, however, experience anxiety because there are various ways to synthesize the psychical and the physical (more colloquially: there are various ways to live). And we are responsible for how we live. Anxiety arises as we work out who we want to be and are overwhelmed by the possibilities and by our responsibility for our actions: "Freedom's possibility announces itself in anxiety" (79).[3] Moreover, there is nothing that tells us definitively how to live.[4] These taken together—our possibilities, our responsibility, and the lack of a definitive "right way" to live—beget anxiety.

But this is not a picture of untethered possibility. He describes anxiety as "entangled freedom," capturing the freedom and the necessity involved in human agency. We can work out how to live within our entanglements and limits (49). By stepping through the entangled freedom of anxiety—by acting and committing ourselves to some paths and not others—we leap from possibility to actuality and become Kierkegaardian selves: it is a leap because how we live is underdetermined by our reasons. We take a stand on (taking responsibility for) the self we will be: "The real 'self' is posited only by the qualitative leap" (79).

This leap of self-responsibility is difficult, however, and there are many ways to avoid it. One way to avoid self-responsibility occurs when one experiences anxiety as fate. In fate, the person fails (or refuses) to recognize her agency. She fails to see (or hides from the fact) that her agency effects change in the world. Kierkegaard uses the image of the oracle to illustrate the necessary and accidental nature of fate. The ambiguity of the oracle's saying allows the person to interpret the saying in different ways with no clearly correct interpretation. The person still acts based on the ambiguous saying, trying to pass responsibility for their actions to the ambiguous saying.

To illustrate fate, Kierkegaard uses the example of the genius, someone who effectively achieves her goals. But when the genius experiences anxiety as fate, they try to pass the responsibility for their actions to the oracle. By relating to their anxiety (and freedom) as fate, the genius stands out:

---

[3] Also: "Anxiety is defined as freedom's disclosure to itself in possibility" (111).
[4] See his discussion of "nothing" in *The Concept of Anxiety* (1980/1844), 76–77.

"he will accomplish astonishing things; nevertheless, he will always succumb to fate" (99). This genius "is dependent on an insignificance that no one comprehends, but upon which the genius grants omnipotence significance" (99). Kierkegaard uses the image of Napoleon longing for the sun of Austerlitz, the day when he defeated both the Austrian and Russian armies. Imagine a modern Napoleon, an athletic genius, who wears the same (unwashed) jersey to keep a win streak alive, unaware of or hiding from the fact that her own genius explains the string of victories, not the foul-smelling jersey. When the streak ends on the day the jersey was mistakenly washed, the superstitious athlete may blame the jersey (or its washer)—with its washed or unwashed status serving as an oracle—for the loss. The blame, however, is misplaced. Whether she would win or lose was always up to her. The washed jersey led to the loss only because she took the omen as determinative of the future. The outward signs are good indicators of what will happen, but only because the genius who succumbs to fate acts based on her interpretation of the oracle's ambiguous saying. She misses the fact that she—not the oracle—determines her actions. Although the genius accomplishes great things, she fails to become a self because, in relating to her anxiety as fate, she is unaware (or hides from the fact) that she is the cause of her actions.

In Chiang's "Anxiety Is the Dizziness of Freedom," various characters respond to the prism technology and the potential awareness of the different lives that paraselves—theirs and others'—could be living. This sometimes causes relief, as it does for Jorge, when he concludes that his slashing his boss' tires was simply an agential hiccup that doesn't reflect anything deep about himself. But awareness of paraselves' lives can lead to regret. If one chooses not to pursue a romantic relationship and ends up lonely, it doesn't help to discover that one's paraself is now deeply happy in that relationship. The story gives a sort of metaphysical reality to the "What if?" questions that naturally follow major, and sometimes minor, decisions. What if I had taken that job, dated that person, moved to that city, and so forth? The prism technology makes these more than purely hypothetical questions, thereby allowing apparently new ways for people to take (or avoid) responsibility for their actions. Dana, Nat, Jorge, and others all grapple with their responsibility, including responsibility for others.

For some, the prisms function much as Kierkegaard's oracle, as they commit to take one path if the prism lights up blue and another path if it lights up red. But like someone who experiences anxiety as fate, despite their best efforts to offload their responsibility for their choices onto the prism, these agents still choose their path. They act based on the red/blue signal, a pronouncement perhaps even more ambiguous than those Kierkegaard describes. And although "few acted so rashly as to commit murder or other felonies … there was a shift in behavior that, while falling short of a mass outbreak of criminality, was readily discernible by social scientists" (311).[5]

Jorge seems inclined to use prisms to avoid taking responsibility for puncturing his manager's tires and, more fundamentally, for whatever in himself would lead him to puncture the tires. When he sends questions to six paraselves and learns that none of them punctured the tires, he is above all relieved. If six different versions of him didn't do it, he tells Dana, "It means that my puncturing his tires was a freak accident. The fact that I did it doesn't say anything important about me as a person" (287). In time, with Dana's guidance, Jorge considers taking responsibility, maybe not by turning himself in to his company but by telling his wife and starting to think about why he did it and, potentially, how to change so that he would be less likely to do similar things in the future.

On the other end of the responsibility spectrum, Dana might be too keenly aware of her responsibility for her actions and of how her choices affect others. Having once lied and blamed her friend to avoid getting in trouble on a school trip, Dana has since spent much of her life dwelling on how her friend Vinessa's life could have gone differently if she had not lied when they had been caught. Although her younger self avoided responsibility and threw Vinessa under the bus, she has since tried to right the wrong, often by offering Vinessa financial help. In her support group, she argues that one's actions matter in this version, even if other versions of yourself will act differently. One's actions, she thinks, are generally consistent with one's character. "Every decision you make contributes to your character and shapes the kind of person you are" (328). Our actions here not only affect ourselves and others in this version, but also the likelihood of future actions, both of this version of ourselves and of versions of ourselves that will split off in the future. "By becoming a better person, you're ensuring that more and more of the branches that split off from this point forward are populated by better versions of you" (329).

In her own life, Dana has taken responsibility for Vinessa's life of delinquency, perhaps to a fault. Ironically, the prism technology ultimately

---

[5] Later, it mentions a statistically significant uptick in crimes of passion (326).

helps her realize the limits of her responsibility for Vinessa.[6] By seeing that Vinessa's life played out in broadly similar ways in many different versions, even when Dana had taken responsibility for the pills on the school trip, Dana realizes that even if she is responsible for her actions, she is not the sole cause of Vinessa's actions.

9.4 Conclusion

For Kierkegaard, every human being must "learn to be anxious in order that he may not perish either never having been in anxiety or by succumbing in anxiety" (155). "Whoever has learned to be anxious in the right way," he writes, "has learned the ultimate" (155). To be educated by anxiety is to be educated by possibility (156), and the prism technology of "Anxiety Is the Dizziness of Freedom" could enable a sort of education by anxiety, by possibility. But it matters how one responds to that education—to neither avoid responsibility for oneself nor to succumb under the weight of that responsibility.[7]

References

Chiang, Ted. 2002. Story of Your Life. In *Stories of Your Life and Others*. New York: Vintage Books.
———. 2019. Anxiety Is The Dizziness of Freedom. In *Exhalation*. New York: Knopf.
Kierkegaard, Soren. 1970. *Soren Kierkegaard's Journals and Papers*, vol. 2 (F–K). Ed. and trans. Howard Hong and Edna Hong. Bloomington, IN: Indiana University Press.
———. 1980/1844 *The Concept of Anxiety*. Trans. Reidar Thomte. Princeton, NJ: Princeton University Press.
Nietzsche, Friedrich. 1974/1887 *The Gay Science*. Trans. Walker Kaufmann. New York: Vintage.

---

[6] The insight comes through Nat's generosity and transformation, who herself had over time learned to better take responsibility for her own actions.
[7] Thanks to Kaia Hathaway and Macy West for their helpful comments on earlier drafts of this chapter.

PART V

Beauty

CHAPTER 10

Just Looking: Check Out the Computational Topography on Her!

Lisa Bellantoni

If beauty is visual cocaine, can—and should—we resist its addictive power? Ted Chiang's story "Liking What You See: A Documentary" explores this question. It imagines a neuroenhancement that defeats "lookism." This tendency, to favor physically attractive people—to judge books by their covers—may be ingrained in our evolutionary psychology. Calliagnosia (Calli) changes that. It allows users to see physical features like eye color or facial proportions objectively, without assigning aesthetic value to them. Thereby, it blunts any "halo effect" that might lead us to unduly attribute positive personality or moral or other social qualities to better looking people, and to favor them in decisions like hiring or romantic partnering. But does Calli really allow us to engage in fairer or what we might term "just" looking, and if so, should we be required to use it?

10.1 Is Beauty Visual Cocaine?

Chiang's story is set on the campus of fictional Pembleton University. An activist group, Students for Equality Everywhere (SEE), is petitioning to require all students to use Calli. Their leader, Maria deSouza, describes it as a tool for developing "assisted maturity": "It lets you do what you know you should: ignore the surface, so you can look deeper."[1] Less physically attractive students are penalized, and more physically attractive students rewarded for something beyond their control. Calli, she suggests, levels that playing field. Here, she takes a *deontological* or duty-based approach to ethical reasoning. For deontologists, all people are equal in their common humanity, independently of their personal qualities or physical traits, and should be treated as such. Relative physical attractiveness is a surface quality irrelevant to one's value and should have no bearing on how we view or treat them.

For deontologists, however, while using Calli might allow us to see individuals more fairly, in their objective moral equality as persons, the foundation of that moral worth is our autonomy, our capacity to make free moral choices. Indeed, our choices have moral worth only when they are freely made. Under SEE's proposal, not only would their classmates be handed a tool that will do their moral labor for them, but they would also be required to use it, though many openly object to doing so.

Fellow Pembleton student Jeff Winthrop, for example, agrees that lookism is unfair. Yet he maintains that "moral maturity" involves seeing the differences among people's appearances and still *recognizing for oneself* that they should not dictate how we treat people. Of moral maturity he says: "There's no technological shortcut."[2] Among ethicists, this point would be echoed by *virtue theorists*, for whom the on-going effort to build our character—our habitual vices and virtues, our "moral maturity"—is the core of our moral lives. On this view, Calli would remove the very struggle and the lengthy learning process through which we forge strong, morally mature decision-making abilities for ourselves.

For both deontological and virtue ethics approaches, Calli poses a similar question: if our technology is doing our moral work for us—if there's an app for that—and inducing or even impelling us to "look fairly" at

---

[1] Chiang, Ted. 2002. Liking What You See: A Documentary. In *Stories of Your Life and Others*, Ted Chiang, 237–75. New York: Vintage Books, p. 238.
[2] Chiang, 247.

people, would this resistance to lookism amount to moral action at all? Would Calli, that is, even be something we could be obliged to use on moral grounds, as SEE proposes in their petition. For another in-story proponent of Calli, Walter Lambert, president of the National Calliagnosia Association, however, the matter is more complicated. "Think of cocaine," he advises his listeners in a speech delivered at the university.[3] In its natural state, it may be pleasurable. Yet once purified and refined, it hits our pleasure receptors with hyper-natural—and addictive—force. Physical beauty is undergoing similar refinement, as advertisers, cosmetic surgeons, air brushers, photo filterers and the like conspire in an ever-expanding race to raise beauty standards. Now, Lambert says: "You've got pharmaceutical-grade beauty, the cocaine of good looks."[4]

10.2 Just Looking?

For Lambert, the physical beauty surrounding Pembleton's students poses a supernormal stimulus, hewing into a visual drug that overwhelms their senses. As a result, the students become ever more dissatisfied with average appearances and ever more prone to over-value exceptional beauty. Not only does this worsen prejudice against unattractive people, making the arbitrary distribution of physical attractiveness and its rewards and penalties even more unfair, but it is not something we can resist unaided. Overwhelmed by more sensory beauty than our brains have evolved to handle, Pembleton students, like all of us, need Calli to defend against such over-stimulation. We cannot develop the moral maturity to evaluate people independently of their looks without it. To treat people fairly, then, to engage in what I'm calling "just looking," Lambert would maintain that we must use Calli whether we wish to our not.

Here, Chiang's story reverses a familiar moral axiom. For most ethicists, we can only be morally obliged to do things that are in our power. If beauty is or functions like an addictive visual drug, if our neurochemistry leaves us powerless to resist it, we could no more be morally obliged to disregard it than to stop breathing or blinking: these actions are not within our voluntary control. Yet what if Calli gave us the power to do something we would otherwise be unable to do, to resist beauty's spell? What if it would allow us to engage in "just looking," focusing on people's

---

[3] Chiang, 250.
[4] Chiang, 250.

objectively observable physical traits, like facial symmetry or proportions—their computational typography, as it were—without ascribing additional aesthetic or other social valuations to them. Are we then morally obligated to use it?

As Chiang's story unfolds, the characters weigh the pleasure of perceiving beauty and enjoying the rewards that accrue to attractive people, against the distressing impact of such judgments upon unbeautiful people. For deontologists, we might not want to give up the perceptual pleasure of seeing attractive people or being regarded as such. But our duty to value and treat all people equally would override our personal preferences. Moreover, deontologists could argue that Calli affects how our brains process visual stimuli, but not the free, rational decisions we make about how to value those perceptions. They could maintain, that is, that Calli would work more like wearing eyeglasses that allow us to see more clearly than like taking a drug that would undermine our free rational judgment. If Calli truly did leave our rational volition or autonomy untouched, while still enabling "just looking," then on deontological grounds we should elect to use it, whether that would be our preference or not.

On these counts, however, for virtue ethicists Calli would still be doing our moral work for us. We might see people more fairly by using it. But we wouldn't become better, more just, people through its use. To the contrary, it would thwart the development of our character, which is the primary goal of our moral actions. At the same time, if Calli leads us to make fairer judgments, does it matter how it does so? For *utilitarians*, it would not. While deontologists and virtue ethicists place primary moral worth on how we make our moral judgments, utilitarians prize the results of our actions. For them, our actions are good when they yield the greatest happiness, the most pleasure, for the greatest number of people and are not good when they fail to maximize that happiness.

As a population, we might find greater total or aggregate pleasure in appreciating beauty, even if its arbitrary distribution disproportionately benefits some individuals over others. Conversely, we might find that we are happier overall dispensing with beauty, withdrawing its privileges from the more attractive, and minimizing any disfavor faced by less attractive people. For utilitarians, whether it is "just" to reward relative attractiveness hinges on whether doing so maximizes aggregate happiness for the total population. If it does, then mandating "just looking" could reduce aggregate happiness and thereby prove unjust.

10.3 What Good Is Beauty?

Here, utilitarians would draw conclusions quite different from deontologists or virtue ethicists. For deontologists, there is no inherent value to pleasure. Both physical beauty and its enjoyment are mere sensual ephemera: at best irrelevant to one's moral judgments, and at worst an impediment to treating people fairly. Surrendering our capacity to enjoy physical attractiveness would be no grave moral loss. Similarly for virtue ethicists, while using Calli might make "just looking" too easy, our capacity to enjoy physical beauty is irrelevant for our moral development and may be a distraction from it. Compared to the moral good of justice, beauty and the pleasure it provides have no comparable moral value.

This point is echoed by SEE leader Maria deSouza. Over the course of our evolution, physical beauty may have cast a powerful spell over our senses. But now, she says, Calli can and should free us from its unjust preeminence: "It's up to us to decide which qualities we value."[5] Physical attractiveness should not be one of those valued qualities, she insists, given its arbitrary and unfair distribution. Nor does Calli take anything of value from us if it prevents us from enjoying the perception of beauty: "All Calli does is keep you from being distracted by surfaces."[6]

The idea that physical attractiveness is merely superficial and dispensable, even morally suspect, echoes throughout Chiang's story and underscores the experience of another Pembleton student, Tamera Lyons. Raised using Calli, she turns it off for the first time when she arrives on campus. She celebrates to discover that she is attractive yet comes to wonder if that attractiveness means she will not be loved "for herself." Maria deSouza voices similar sentiments: "True beauty is what you see with the eyes of love."[7] To see with the eyes of love, she says, we require the moral progress that Calli allows: "I say that physical beauty is something we no longer need."[8]

The endeavor to "outgrow" physical beauty, and to see beyond mere appearance to value people in themselves, animates SEE's battle against lookism. But suppose we—do—look beyond that surface, what selves do we find there? What is it that we value in favored friends and partners beyond their appearance? Their personality? Their voice? Their

---

[5] Chiang, 268.
[6] Chiang, 269.
[7] Chiang, 269.
[8] Chiang, 268.

intelligence? Their wit? Their warmth? SEE proponents like Maria deSouza insist that we are *more* our personal qualities, like humor or intelligence or extraversion or kindness, than we are our physical appearances; that those qualities are legitimately or truly our "selves" in ways our surface appearances are not. But how is that the case?

According to SEE's representatives, we are not our appearances because we didn't freely select them. Moreover, we should not be judged on these appearances because they are arbitrarily valued, and because favored ones are distributed unfairly, independently of our equal moral worth. Yet these descriptions hold equally for all the other qualities that lead us to favor—to befriend, even to love—some individuals rather than others. Maybe it is unjust to love one person rather than another because the first is more physically attractive. But what if we love that favored person instead because they are funnier or more extraverted, more intelligent, or more kind?

We value these qualities, after all, much like we value beauty, because they are *pleasing to us*. Moreover, these qualities are not distributed fairly, or prized equally, or even chosen freely by us. Pretty people may have unfair social advantages. But what about witty people, or charismatic people, or natural leaders? Do we treat people unfairly anytime we prize some personal qualities over others? Worse, if we are directed to love people "for themselves," but those selves are composed of pleasing qualities which, like beauty, are unfairly distributed and arbitrarily and unequally prized, wouldn't such love, like lookism, prove an immoral favoritism?

The point of Calli, of course, is to reduce unjust favoritism by masking beauty; this, we're told, will allow us to see people "as themselves," and thereby, to look at them fairly. But on SEE's account seeing people fairly would require even more. It would demand that we overlook all qualities which arbitrarily please us, insofar as those qualities, too, are unfairly acquired and unevenly prized and prompt unjust favoritisms. That masking might indeed make for a fairer society. Wiping away these pleasing qualities, however, seems less likely to reveal people "as themselves" than to negate them, draining away their individuality and their distinctive import to us. Moreover, for utilitarians, if these qualities like wit, or warmth, or intelligence, or kindness, or charisma—or beauty—are sources of pleasure, then blotting them out poses a significant moral cost, a loss of value. Indeed, the demand that we mask them to engage in "just looking" would itself prove a significant injustice, minimizing rather than maximizing our aggregate happiness.

10.4 Fetishizing Fairness

In the end SEE's proposal is defeated. What ultimately seems to sway the student vote against requiring the use of Calli on campus is a broad-casted speech given by Rebecca Boyer, a spokesperson for PEN (People for Ethical Nanomedicine). Originally posing as a grass roots public interest group, PEN turns out to be a campaign funded by cosmetics companies to oppose the adoption of technologies like Calli. Boyer's broadcast, moreover, seems to have been manipulated by an even newer digital technology that enhances not only speakers' appearances but their voices, facial expressions, body language, and charisma, all aimed at optimizing viewers' emotional responses.

As an in-story critic, neurologist Walter Lambert, reports, this technology creates another hyper stimulation "like flawless beauty but even more dangerous."[9] Faced with relentless manipulation by models that appear too beautiful, politicians that appear too persuasive and salespeople that appear too charismatic, we will all need additional neuroenhancements. These enhancements, like Calli, will presumably work by draining these stimuli, too, of their perceptual force—leaving words with no tone, faces with no aesthetic properties, voices with no emotive force.

But to what end? These proposed technologies might induce new varieties of "just looking," just as Calli replaces aesthetic responses with disinterested observations, and drain yet more unjust elements from our perceptions. Here, we might even grant the whole of SEE's case: we may illicitly fetishize beauty, we may be biologically predisposed, even addicted to it, and defenseless against its intoxication; and we almost surely treat people unfairly on these bases. Maybe it is a measure of our moral immaturity, our inability to engage in "just looking," that technologies like Calli will be needed and increasingly so. Mandating Calli, however, implies not only that acting on our preferences is unjust, for example, in preferentially hiring pretty people, but that the preferences themselves are unjust and that we can wrong someone morally with a mere glance. Is that really what we do, whenever our eyes sweep a room, and settle on an attractive face? More pointedly, is that really something we are morally obliged to do without, in the interests of justice?

For SEE proponents, that question may not matter. It may be that the mere noticing of attractiveness irresistibly bleeds into how we treat people,

---

[9] Chiang, 272.

unconsciously favoring some over others for something as arbitrary and ephemeral as physical beauty. But beauty is one of many such individualizing traits, like wit, and warmth, and charisma, which are distributed arbitrarily, and prized unequally, and factored haphazardly into the equations that decide who we favor and who we love. As the ending of Chiang's story hints, many of these qualities may prove subject to enhancement, in an ever-spiraling arms race to curry social favor. In that case, blinding us to beauty, as Calli proposes, *might* lead to more fair treatment. Yet it could just as readily redirect our attention to other arbitrarily appealing traits, illicitly magnifying *their* import in our social exchanges. The idea that we can, or should, or must wipe away these qualities to value the "real people" underneath, i.e., that we must value people independently of all these superficially pleasing qualities—of which beauty is but one—seems basically muddled. Whatever else we are, we are our covers, just as we are sums of our other ephemeral qualities that are no less arbitrarily distributed and unfairly prized than beauty.

To that extent, lookism—and its purported cure in Calli—may signal another moral challenge entirely. Calli might prove a boon to fairness, to what I've called "just looking." Still, the vexing question remains whether fairness is the ultimate good decisive here. Maybe it should thrill us, the prospect that we could make ostensibly moral choices more easily. Maybe we could do with a little less autonomy, so long as we get our moral choices right. Maybe we could live with a world less lovely, if only it were more fair. Against the dispiriting reality of lookism, however, Calli poses an even more chilling prospect: to see the world more fairly, we will be blinded to it. Is stripping the world of beauty, in the interests of making it more fair, moral progress?

Chiang's story presents Calliagnosia as a neuroenhancement. Yet how can that be when, as one central character, neurologist Joseph Weingartner describes it: "Inducing an agnosia means simulating a specific brain lesion."[10] Calli depicts simulating brain damage as *enhancement*, as if voluntarily deadening our senses might somehow bring us to them. Maybe, as SEE's petition insists, we do need to go this far, to improve our moral vision. Maybe we should be required to use Calli, to ensure that we stop

---

[10] Chiang, 244.

fetishizing beauty and engage in "just looking." SEE's quest, however, seems instead to fetishize fairness and unjustly so. How much can justice legitimately demand of us? Maybe not this much. What good is seeing the world fairly, after all, if in the process we're not really seeing it at all?

CHAPTER 11

Should You Like What You See? Ethics, Aesthetics, and the Appreciation of Human Beauty

Alyssa Izatt and Julia Minarik

> Was this the face that launch'd a thousand ships,And burnt the topless towers of Ilium—Sweet Helen, make me immortal with a kiss.
> —Christopher Marlowe, Dr. Faustus

> For the moon never beams,
> without bringing me dreams of the beautiful Annabel Lee;
> And the stars never rise, but I feel the bright eyes of the beautiful Annabel Lee;
> —Edgar Allan Poe, Annabel Lee

A. Izatt (✉)
Vancouver, BC, Canada
e-mail: alyssaji@student.ubc.ca

J. Minarik
Toronto, ON, Canada
e-mail: julia.minarik@mail.utoronto.ca

© The Author(s), under exclusive license to Springer Nature Switzerland AG 2025
D. Friedell (ed.), *The Philosophy of Ted Chiang*,
https://doi.org/10.1007/978-3-031-81662-8_11

11.1 Liking What You See

Tamera Lyons doesn't experience human beauty. She has been raised with calliagnosia (or "calli"), a technology which prevents her from recognizing whether someone is attractive or unattractive. In "Liking What You See: a Documentary," Ted Chiang imagines a world in which the perception of human beauty is optional (Chiang 2010). Some characters in Chiang's world embrace calli wholeheartedly, viewing the technology as a new frontier for equality and empowerment, and a solution for preventing discrimination and harm based on looks; calli is an "assisted maturity" that allows one to "ignore the surface and look deeper." Others reject calli, for them, beauty is worth the risk—an encounter with beauty is one of the most joyful human experiences and to give it up is to give up on something rich and wonderful. If it is wrong to enjoy the beauty of others, we can no longer admire the beautiful face of a photograph's subject, the allure of Mona Lisa's smile, or the electric appearances of our favorite actors and actresses. So we choose the ability to experience beauty or easy morality? It is one of the world's great misfortunes that our moral and aesthetic interests appear to be so incompatible.

Chiang's story expertly reflects on this misfortune; this tension between our moral and aesthetic interests. He shows us how our captivation with human beauty causes us to do morally bad things. We objectify those we find beautiful, and lookism—discrimination based on appearance—harms those that are deemed to be ugly or unattractive. At the same time Chiang reminds us of beauty's experiential value. Our aim is to analyze this tension (where does it come from?) and propose a way to reconcile these competing ends. We suggest that we discriminate in part because we blend our moral and aesthetic values. Optimistically, we suggest that provided the right moral and aesthetic attention, people can combat this blending without calli. We argue that it is not unethical to admire a person's beauty, if the observer also pays proper attention to that person's moral character. Indeed, this enjoyment of beauty can be virtuous because beauty takes us outside of ourselves, reminding us of the value of other people, and inspiring us to widely recognize, preserve, and appreciate that value. Seeing beauty in this way should make it at least possible to combat the development of lookist or sexist attitudes.

11.2 "Beauty Is What Blinds You."

There are at least two kinds of look-based discrimination: lookism and objectification. Lookism can be summarized as the claim that we like and value beautiful people more than others simply because they are beautiful. The evidence is undeniable: attractive people are more likely to be hired and are paid more when they are (Hoffman 2023); receive preferential treatment from the justice system (Berry 2019); hold higher status among their peers (Yarosh 2019); and are literally *seen as* more intelligent, credible, and trustworthy (Spiegel 2023). Tamera's reflections on beautiful men after removing her calli are chilling: "After I looked at him for a while, I found it really easy to imagine that he was a nice guy! I didn't know anything about him." Objectification, unlike lookism, does not involve attributing more value to the objectified because of their beauty; instead, it involves taking their value to lie *entirely within* their beauty. Often objectification manifests as women being treated as mere objects for male pleasure with little to no other value. Jolene Carter worries about this in Chiang's story. She says: "Whenever I like a guy, I always wonder how much he's interested in me, versus how much he's interested in my looks."

Both forms of discrimination exemplify beauty overtaking other values—either by making us think (without good reason) that other values are present or by supplanting these other values entirely. Like Tamera, we regularly fail to understand our valuations of others; we take aesthetic value (beauty) to indicate the presence of other value, and aesthetic disvalue (ugliness) to indicate other lacks. Being beautiful (or ugly) makes you *seem to be* more (or less) moral, intelligent, and able—despite providing no evidence for any of these traits. Call this "value-blending."

According to Ferrari et al. (2017) we do in fact value-blend and might value-blend because beauty and morality exploit a common neural network in the brain. This value-blending (and supplanting) is bad because it means that we are valuing people *for the wrong reasons*. The presence of beauty in an object signals to us the presence of reasons why it is beautiful: if a painting is beautiful, it is because it has features that make it so (Lopes 2018). When we blend our aesthetic and moral values, we end up wrongly attributing moral value to someone *for aesthetic reasons*. In other words, we end up valuing people as kind or intelligent beings because they have symmetrical faces with clear, youthful skin (Hoffman 2023)—instead of valuing their actual kindness or intelligence. The unfortunate result is that a person's value ends up significantly determined by their beauty rather than in other traits that are more praiseworthy. As Rachel Lyons reminds us, "being pretty is fundamentally a passive quality; even when you work at it, you're working at being passive." When we appreciate someone's facial beauty, we do not honor them for something achieved; instead, we honor them for their genetic luck.

To make matters worse, beautiful people are easier to look at and we *want* to look at them more because of this ease. Beautiful people are literally easier to pay attention to because beauty facilitates attention (Matthen 2017; Sui & Liu 2009). Tamera watches the video of the girl in the advertisement over and over: "I just stood there and watched the commercial like five times, just so I could look at her some more." What this means is that beauty distracts us from other values. This should make us wonder whether beauty is worth it. Monroe Beardsley in his 1968 presidential address to the American Society for Aesthetics captures this worry nicely: "When so many of us in this troubled land do not seem to care very much, even for one another ... the aesthetic point of view becomes difficult to sustain. It may even seem absurd" (Beardsley 1969). Although Beardsley was asking why we should care about studying aesthetics at all, his comments are apt here: why admire human beauty when it seems to prevent us from equitably caring for and properly valuing each other? What do we get by appreciating the beauty of another?

11.3 Calliagnosia

The proponent of Calliagnosia makes a bold promise to free us from physical temptation and therefore moral transgression. To turn on Calli is to free oneself from *facial* beauty. Of course, it is also to lose a rich part of the human experience: what inspires Andrew Marvell without his coy mistress, or Poe without his Annabel Lee? Does ethics demand of us a life lived free of the heart-melting beauty of a partner's eyes? Perhaps we are too idealistic to think that our experience of beautiful faces can be preserved without any harmful consequences, but we hope for a life well-balanced. There are, we think, at least two reasons to try and preserve facial beauty: (1) it's not clear that facial beauty is the primary cause of discriminatory attitudes and (2) beauty inspires us.

As morally noble as they are, Chiang reminds us that the proponent of Calliagnosia is too optimistic: "Calliagnosics are *not* blind to fashion or cultural standards of beauty. If black lipstick is all the rage, calliagnosia won't make you forget it … So calliagnosia by itself can't eliminate appearance-based discrimination … it takes away the innate predisposition, the tendency for such discrimination to arise in the first place." Calliagnosia cannot prevent our socially conditioned and media-shaped beauty standards, such as weight-based, ability-based, and racial standards. Calli prevents us from seeing beauty in general, but as long as we see beauty in general, there will be the potential for discrimination based on it, all calli has done is eliminate one source. The causes of visual discrimination are complex; many forms of visual discrimination such as fat oppression are, *to a significant degree*, caused by *pernicious and highly fixed* false beliefs about fat people (Irvin 2017), rather than assessments of beauty (although these beliefs lead us to then evaluate fat people as non-beautiful). Although we hear about children with burn scars being successful in Chiang's story, we do not hear how the fat children fare. Chiang recognizes this when he concludes his story with the dystopian suggestion that we might need to implement other agnosias in the future, such as an agnosia that prevents us from hearing tones of voice in order to avoid being unjustly persuaded by good speakers.

Second, beauty, despite its risks, also incites us to love and create. Elaine Scarry (1999) claims that beauty calls us outside of ourselves, reminding us of the value of others, and psychological research has suggested that being in an aesthetically pleasing environment can increase one's moral behavior (Wu and He 2021). Furthermore, beauty calls us to preserve it and to multiply it: "beautiful persons and things incite the desire to create" (Scarry, 77). Think of the arts we would lose that rely on human beauty: such as portraiture, makeup, sculpture, the poems quoted at the start, aspects of fashion, etc. As Rachel notes, with Calliagnosia, "there's something you can't see." The more beauty in the world, the more potential for value, inspiration, and joy. If we can preserve beauty, there is good reason to think that we should.

11.4 Aesthetics and Attention

We do not need agnosia to fight the negative aspects of our encounters with beautiful people—we can also do this by properly directing our attention. We pay attention to different things depending on our motivations, actions, and surroundings. A person crossing the street focuses their attention more closely on passing cars and bikes than a person who is walking on the sidewalk; a student taking an exam might have their attention directed unwillingly to the construction worker loudly drilling on the floor above them. Not all of the ways we direct our attention are deliberate, but oftentimes, we are able to influence our attention. *Moral attention* plays an important role in how to engage with others in the right way. Famously, Iris Murdoch (1970) argued that to engage with others virtuously, we must attend to their moral character. The virtuous person recognizes the other as a person like themselves and does not allow for external factors to impede this recognition. If another person is noticeably in distress, an attentive person will recognize this and respond appropriately. This means that attention is important both for how we engage with others as individuals and how we morally behave, since the appropriate direction of attention is necessary for both. Take the example of an attractive young woman who is treated as incompetent by her boss, despite her good performance at work. He underestimates her, because he allows his perception of her beauty to negatively impact his judgment of her as a person and as an employee. In other words, he does not pay attention to her for the right reasons. Murdoch would deem this to be a failure of appropriate attention, since in admiring her appearance, the employer does not recognize his employee's moral character or the characteristics that define her as an individual.

We propose that in order to morally like what we see, we should attend to a person's moral character in addition to, and often over, their physical appearance. Otherwise, we do something morally bad. This means that in appreciating the beauty of a passerby on the street, we must also at once recognize her as a member of the moral community. Delineating these two types of value judgment—moral and aesthetic—and ensuring that our moral assessment is not biased by our aesthetic assessment, are important in avoiding the ways in which sexism and lookism can implicitly direct our attention. Given that lookist and sexist norms permeate our society, changing how we focus on other people will require deliberate intervention. We must ensure that how we attend to other people is not compromised by our aesthetic judgments. This is no small task. Indeed, look-based discrimination does not seem to be a product of deliberate judgment. It happens automatically and is difficult to combat (Sui & Liu 2009). This is why it is apt that we change our *attention*. By being conscientious about how we direct our moral assessments, we can attend to qualities of a person that might otherwise be ignored, due to lookist prejudices. As we continue to direct our attention in such a way and habituate our attention, these features will become increasingly noticeable—attending to others in the right way will become easier.

So, in cases of lookism and objectification, part of what is going wrong is how we pay moral attention to others. Our aesthetic perceptions influence which moral and personal qualities we recognize when we engage with other people, and this can lead to poor holistic assessments. For instance, as in the cases of look-based discrimination, negative aesthetic judgments about an employee's size can lead to an assessment of the employee as incompetent and lazy. To engage with the aesthetic qualities of others, we need to be careful that our moral attention takes precedence over our aesthetic attention and that aesthetic judgments do not hinder our ability to recognize the moral character of others. Our aesthetic engagement with others should also be accompanied by suitable moral attention. In admiring the beauty of one's partner, one should also be recognizing them for their relevant moral qualities, for instance, their compassion or their loyalty.

11.5 The Choice

In Chiang's story, as a part of the students' adherence to the college's Code of Ethical Conduct, a group of activists on Tamera's campus campaign to make calli mandatory for students. They argue that calliagnosia is the way forward in promoting equitable treatment of students on campus. In contrast, we propose that the students are not obligated to turn on calliagnosia. Indeed, there will be some aesthetic losses when they blind themselves to the beauty of others. Turning on calliagnosia would mean that we lose the aesthetic value that the appreciation of human beauty adds to our lives, and thus lose a joyful human experience. As a result, our engagement with art is diminished, as is our well-being, to a degree.

However, not having calliagnosia comes with some serious attentional obligations. We must separate our moral and aesthetic judgments, and recognize how they so often run together. We should cultivate new attentional patterns, in order to properly recognize those we interact with. In other words, we can like what we see, so long as it does not compromise our moral recognition of others. Our moral attention is most often compromised in this way. Further, cultivating these uncompromised attentional patterns is no doubt challenging and may yield varying degrees of success, especially since judgments about attractiveness and beauty happen very fast (Luoto 2017). If a person is unwilling or unable to do this work, then calliagnosia, despite the aesthetic and prudential losses it will cause, would be the best solution. Indeed, there may be instances, such as the workplace, where calliagnosia is beneficial, since the aesthetic admiration of one's colleagues is often unwarranted. Despite the challenges we face without calliagnosia, the difficulty of cultivating our attention is alone not a reason to give up the pursuit. In the same way that challenging racist or sexist biases is difficult and emotionally demanding, challenging our lookist biases will take a lot of effort. Ultimately though, we will be better, as individuals and as moral agents, for having done the work.

For the characters in Chiang's story, calliagnosia presents a true dilemma. They can lose a dimension of beauty, or they can try (and perhaps fail) to recognize each other without their lookist biases. We think that the cultivation of moral attention is worth the effort. The choice, however, is up to them. As for the rest of us who are as of yet without calli, there is a lot of attentional work left to do.

References

Beardsley, Monroe C. 1969. Aesthetic Experience Regained. *The Journal of Aesthetics and Art Criticism* 28 (1): 3–11. https://doi.org/10.2307/428903.

Berry, Bonnie, ed. 2019. *Appearance Bias and Crime*. Cambridge: Cambridge University Press. https://doi.org/10.1017/9781108377683.

Chiang, Ted. 2010. Liking What You See: A Documentary. In *Stories of Your Life and Others*. Knopf Doubleday Publishing Group.

Ferrari, Chiara, et al. 2017. The Dorsomedial Prefrontal Cortex Mediates the Interaction between Moral and Aesthetic Valuation: A TMS Study on the Beauty-Is-Good Stereotype. *Social Cognitive and Affective Neuroscience* 12 (5): 707–717. https://doi.org/10.1093/scan/nsx002.

Hofmann, Bjørn. 2023. March 31, Aesthetic Injustice. *Journal of Business Ethics*. https://doi.org/10.1007/s10551-023-05401-4.

Irvin, Sherri. 2017. Resisting Body Oppression: An Aesthetic Approach. *Feminist Philosophy Quarterly* 3 (4): 1–26.

Lopes, Dominic Mc Iver. 2018. *Being for Beauty*. Oxford University Press.

Luoto, Severi. 2017. Commentary: Beauty Requires Thought. *Frontiers in Psychology* 8. https://www.frontiersin.org/articles/10.3389/fpsyg.2017.01281.

Matthen, Mohan. 2017. The Pleasure of Art. *Australasian Philosophical Review* 1 (1): 6–28.

Murdoch, Iris. 1970. *The Sovereignty of Good*. Routledge.

Scarry, Elaine. 1999. *On Beauty and Being Just*. Princeton University Press.

Spiegel, Thomas J. 2023. Lookism as Epistemic Injustice. *Social Epistemology* 37 (1): 47–61. https://doi.org/10.1080/02691728.2022.2076629.

Sui, Jie, and Chang Hong Liu. 2009. Can Beauty Be Ignored? Effects of Facial Attractiveness on Covert Attention. *Psychonomic Bulletin & Review* 16 (2): 276–281. https://doi.org/10.3758/PBR.16.2.276.

Wu, Chenjing, and Xianyou He. 2021. Environmental Aesthetic Value Influences the Intention for Moral Behavior: Changes in Behavioral Moral Judgment. *International Journal of Environmental Research and Public Health* 18 (12): 6477. https://doi.org/10.3390/ijerph18126477.

Yarosh, Daniel B. 2019. Perception and Deception: Human Beauty and the Brain. *Behavioral Sciences* 9 (4): 34. https://doi.org/10.3390/bs9040034.

PART VI

Procreation Ethics

CHAPTER 12

The Ethics of Making a Short Life

Audrey Benson and Mayah Teplitskiy

12.1 INTRODUCTION

From early childhood we are ingrained with the same story of a "typical life." We are supposed to get a good education, find a job, get married, start a family, work until we are ready to retire, and one day it all comes to an end. That's a life many people lead, and although it is becoming more acceptable to break out of this typical life, a lot of people still want it. There are many reasons to live life following this path. Many of us want families because we want our lives to be filled with people who love us and people we can love. We need money and therefore jobs, and the requisite education to support our families. And so, we often end up falling into this familiar routine, following the same life path of so many others.

The characters in Ted Chiang's "Story of Your Life" follow this path as well. But, this novella also raises questions about the very beginning of this chain that many of us have been pressured to follow: procreation. In

---

A. Benson (✉)
Schenectady, NY, USA
e-mail: bensona2@union.edu

M. Teplitskiy
Brighton, MA, USA
e-mail: mayahtep@gmail.com

"Story of Your Life," aliens called heptapods come to Earth. Louise is a linguist who learns the languages heptapods speak and write in, called Heptapod A and Heptapod B, respectively. While communicating with the heptapods, Lousie learns to experience time as the heptapods do. "Occasionally I have glimpses when Heptapod B truly reigns, and I experience past and future all at once" (35). During these glimpses Louise learns that she will have a child who will live a normal life but will fall off a cliff while rock climbing and die at twenty-five years old. Yet, when her husband at the time, Gary, asks if Louise wants to make a baby, she embraces the future and answers yes.

Louise's decision to embrace creating her daughter who will die a tragic death at a very young age raises several philosophical questions: Louise can't change the future she has already seen to be true, but is she doing something wrong by embracing it? How different are we from Louise? There are some extreme cases where it's known that a child will die soon after being born and will suffer for the extent of life that they live. But even outside of these extreme cases, suffering is still a part of life. When we choose to have children, we know that at some point or another they will suffer and at some point they will die. Knowing this, is it wrong of us to choose to have children anyway?

Philosophers have taken many different stances on the ethics behind having children when we know they will suffer. Before discussing these stances, it is important to note the distinction between something being *morally required, morally permissible,* and *morally impermissible.* If something is morally required, then you have a duty to do it. So, for example, if you are hiking a mountain trail that passes by a river and you see a child drowning in the river with nobody else around, you might think that you are morally required to pull the child out of the river. When something is morally impermissible, it means that you have a moral responsibility to *not* do it. For example, you have a moral responsibility to *not* taunt the drowning child. And then, something morally permissible is something that you do not have a moral responsibility to do, but you also do not have a moral responsibility not to do it. So, you might think it is not morally required for you to teach the child how to swim (after saving their life), but it is also not morally impermissible for you to teach the child how to swim. It's up to you, morally speaking.

This distinction allows us to discuss in more depth the morality of not only Louise's decision to embrace the fate of her future child but also our choice to have children when we know that they will suffer.

12.2 Anti-natalism

A natural stance on the ethics of procreation is that it is morally permissible—you aren't required to have children, but you also aren't required to not have children. A more striking philosophical view is anti-natalism, the view that procreating is always (or often) morally impermissible. That is, the view that we have a moral responsibility to not procreate. There are many different ways that philosophers argue for this controversial view, though they generally seem to fall into two categories, *philanthropic* or *misanthropic*.

A philanthropic argument for anti-natalism focuses on the harm that would be inflicted upon the individual if they were brought into the world. One of the most prominent anti-natalists, the philosopher David Benatar, argues that everyone who is brought into the world is harmed by their birth, and so, bringing someone into the world immorally harms them.[1] Benatar thinks even those of us who are lucky enough to live ordinary lives free of extreme hardship and oppression—a life largely unaffected by, for example, war or slavery—do not live lives worth living. The pains of even an ordinary life outweigh the pleasures. We lose family members to disease and aging. We experience deep heartbreaks in our personal and professional lives. In addition to these epic and dramatic pains, life also has a ton of mundane, everyday pains: thirst, hunger, tiredness, boredom, itches, leaky faucets, and annoyances. Pessimistically, Benatar concludes that even if you're lucky enough to live a life you think is worth living, you're deluded. Life sucks, according to Benatar.

A *misanthropic* argument for anti-natalism defends the stance that it is unethical to bring someone into the world—not because life would be bad for *them*, but because of the harm it will cause the environment around them. Benatar argues that humans are inherently destructive in the way that they interact with other humans, animals, and the environment around them, and due to the pain and suffering humans cause, we have a moral responsibility to not procreate. You might think your future child will be a gift to the world, but chances are, according to Benatar, they will not.

There is also an argument for anti-natalism that focuses on the consent of the person being born. There was recently a controversial video posted

---

[1] Our understanding of Benatar relies on his work (2006) and subsequent discussion by the philosopher Elizabeth Harman (2009).

on TikTok where a woman claimed she had sued her parents for giving birth to her without her consent. She essentially argued that because her parents did not ask her for her permission to be born, they should be required to pay for her and support her throughout her entire life. It later came out that she was joking and that her account on TikTok was actually meant to be satirical, but her argument is very much in line with the consent argument for anti-natalism. On this argument, it is morally impermissible for us to procreate because children cannot consent to being born, and it is wrong to give birth to a child without their consent.

12.3 Objections to Anti-natalism and a Proposal

A feminist objection to anti-natalism focuses on the feminist philosophy of bodily autonomy.[2] Declaring that it is morally impermissible to have children denies child-bearing individuals autonomy over their bodies. The feminist objection also applies to the idea that having children is morally required. If having children is morally required, then new expectations are created that may coerce child-bearing individuals to pursue fertility treatments or to feel pressured to have children when they do not want to or are not healthy enough. Therefore, feminist perspectives on procreative autonomy generally promote procreation as being morally permissible. This empowers child-bearing individuals to decide what happens to their bodies and does not put pressure on them to subject themselves to medical treatments or to child birth if they do not want to or cannot have children.

Another objection to anti-natalism, the preservation of humanity objection, focuses on the effects of adopting anti-natalism. Misanthropic arguments for anti-natalism suggest that humans are bad to each other and to the environment, and so we should not bring more people into the world. However, if we stop bringing people into the world, then humanity would quickly die out. The preservation of humanity objection promotes the idea that although humans may be harmful to each other and to the environment, it would still be bad for humanity to completely die out.

A common objection to Benatar is that although we suffer during our lives, most people are not deluded when they think their lives are worth

---

[2] A discussion of the feminist objection to anti-natalism, as well as several other objections can be found in the Parenthood and Procreation section of the Stanford Encyclopedia of Philosophy, https://plato.stanford.edu/entries/parenthood/.

living. Life, with its ups and downs, is valuable and beautiful. Cheer up, Benatar! Although it's true that sometimes life can have moments of suffering, it's rather pessimistic to throw up our hands and presume then that life is not worth living. There is much more to life than the sadness we may face in it. In fact, for many of us, it seems as though the good moments in life outweigh the bad. This suggests that, all things considered, it is morally permissible (but not required) to bring someone into existence if they are likely to have a good life—and we think that many people do, in fact, live good lives. We think Benatar is too pessimistic.

12.4 Ethics of Louise's Decision

The situation raised in "Story of Your Life" is not a typical situation of choosing to have a child. Louise knows that she gives birth to a daughter who dies in a tragic accident at twenty-five years old, and she still embraces the birth of her daughter. So, although anti-natalists might be uncomfortable with Louise *embracing* the future birth, there is a philosophically serious complication: given that Louise knows and experiences the future all at once, she's deeply different from those of us who might ordinarily choose to procreate. Does Louise, given her literally alien psychology, even have free will? And if not, is there any sense in which her decisions to do *anything*, let alone embrace and create her future daughter's life, can be morally impermissible?

Even setting aside these big questions about Louise's free will (or lack thereof), there's a further complication. Before, we discussed a proposal that it's morally permissible to bring someone into the world that is likely to live a good life. What exactly makes a life good? In "Story of Your Life," not only does Louise's divorce with her husband Gary deeply affect their daughter, but Louise's daughter's death is also painful. So, there are several causes of extreme pain that happen in her daughter's short life. But, her daughter also experiences so many joys—going on family vacations, graduating from college, and climbing anything from jungle gyms on a playground to cliff faces in national parks, just to name a few. Do the pleasures in her life outweigh the suffering? And, if so, does that mean that Louise's decision to embrace having a child is morally permissible?

Louise knows everything that will happen during her daughter's life. And, although many of the snippets of her life that we see involve suffering, Louise also knows the pleasures her daughter will experience. So, according to our proposal, if Louise knows that her daughter will experience so much pleasure that it will outweigh her pain, then it is morally permissible to have that child. And therefore, her embracing having a child is also morally permissible. If, on the other hand, Louise knows that the pain and suffering in her daughter's life will outweigh the amount of pleasure she experiences, it would be morally impermissible for Louise to have the child and, therefore, morally impermissible to embrace having the child.

12.5　Our Likeness to Louise

What implications, if any, does this assessment of the ethics behind Louise's choice have for our decisions to have children? It is important to emphasize that we are not in the same position as Louise. We know that our children will suffer and experience pain at some points in life. We know that our children will die one day. But, we do not know everything that will happen to our children and we, generally, do not know when they will die before we have them. Louise knows whether or not her child's life will be good, and so there is a clear stance on whether or not Louise having a child is morally permissible or impermissible.

In our case, we do not know what will happen to our children. So, the question becomes whether or not we can somehow fall into the case of believing that our children are likely to live a life in which the suffering is outweighed by pleasure. It is reasonable to think that it is not possible for us to fall into this case. We can be sure that good things will happen to our children. For example, if you have enough money, you can be sure that you will be able to buy a toy for your child. However, we cannot be sure of how much suffering our children will experience compared to the amount of pleasure. If our children, for instance, experience several small pleasures (like being bought a toy), but no large pleasures, then any single extremely painful experience may outweigh the collective sum of pleasure.

Another issue is that there is no reason to think that we can prevent our children from having even a single extremely painful experience. In fact, it is almost certain to happen. From getting sick, to heartbreak, to losing loved ones, there are many difficult things that happen in life, almost guaranteeing extreme pain. Extreme pleasure, although very much possible, is definitely not a guarantee. So, it does not ever seem reasonable to believe that our children will have good lives. Therefore, even the philanthropic arguments for anti-natalism would suggest that it is always morally impermissible for us to have children.

Whether or not it is reasonable for us to believe that our children will have lives in which the pleasure outweighs the suffering, most people who have children still do think their children will have good lives. That is one of the factors that goes into many people's decisions to have children. Are we ready to have a child? Can we financially support the child? Can we give the child a good life? Even if it is right that these parents are being unreasonable, they still think they are doing something morally permissible.

12.6 Ethics of Short Lives

Chiang's novella raises an even trickier question. We all know our children will die. We hope that they will live long lives full of happiness, but unfortunately many children, like Louise's daughter, die young. Can we still say that these children have lived good lives if they have only lived very short lives? If not, then perhaps this should make us more cautious about procreating, knowing that there's a chance our children will live short lives.

We propose that as long as the pleasures in life outweigh the suffering, short lives, just as long lives, are worth living and can be good lives. What matters is not length, but quality. After all, Ted Chiang writes short stories. Does their length make them less worthy of being read or written than long stories? Perhaps, the fact that they are short makes them worth reading and writing even more.

Acknowledgments Thanks to David Friedell for helpful comments and support.

References

Benatar, David. 2006. *Better never to have been: The harm of coming into existence.* Oxford, NY: Clarendon Press; Oxford University Press.

Harman, Elizabeth. 2009. David Benatar. Better Never to Have Been: The Harm of Coming into Existence. *Noûs* 43:776–785. https://doi.org/10.1111/j.1468-0068.2009.00727.x.

PART VII

Contradictions

CHAPTER 13

Knowledge, Symbols, and Understanding

Kenny Easwaran

Like in any human endeavor, there are different kinds of knowledge one can have in mathematics. Someone reliable tells you that something is true, and you believe it, and this gives you a basic kind of knowledge. Or you work things out using a method you know to be reliable and convince yourself that this thing must be true. But most satisfying is when you manage to understand *why* it is true, by seeing the claim in a light that makes it clear that it *had* to be true. Ted Chiang's story, "Division by Zero", is about the destabilizing effect that occurs when this deepest level of knowledge is undone.

13.1 I.

Let's illustrate these different levels of knowledge with an example. There is a formula that you may or may not remember from an algebra class, that $b^2 - a^2 = (b + a)(b - a)$. That is, for any two numbers, a and b, the difference between their squares, b^2 and a^2, is a number that can be factored into the difference of the two numbers and the sum of the two numbers.

Assuming you trust me, or remember from an algebra class, you now have the first level of knowledge of the truth of this equation.

You can get a deeper level of knowledge by seeing the algebraic reasoning yourself. (Or you can skip the next two paragraphs to avoid the algebraic formalism and go directly to the geometric understanding, or skip all the way to the next section if you are happy remaining at the level of pure trust, both about the mathematical result and about the way the different levels of mathematical knowledge feel.)

We can start with the right side of the equation, $(b + a)(b - a)$, and expand it algebraically. This is a multiplication of two quantities formed by addition and subtraction, so we can apply the distributive rule of multiplication. Applying it to the left term, if you add two things together and then multiply by something else, the result must be the same as multiplying each of the two terms by that thing and then doing the addition, so $(b + a) \times (b - a) = b \times (b - a) + a \times (b - a)$. Each of the resulting terms is now something times a difference of two terms, and so this is the same as multiplying that thing by each term and then take the difference, yielding $(b \times b - a \times b) + (b \times a - a \times a)$. Looking at the middle two terms, the commutative rule tells us that $a \times b = b \times a$, so since one of them is negative and the other is positive, they must cancel. Thus, $(b + a)(b - a) = b \times b - a \times a$. But this term on the right just is what $b^2 - a^2$ means, so we have verified that the equation must hold.

So far, this is just a mechanical use of the formalism of algebra. If we've understood the rules of how the terms can be manipulated, we can use them to verify that the result is correct. But we still don't have a deep, intuitive understanding of it.

13 KNOWLEDGE, SYMBOLS, AND UNDERSTANDING

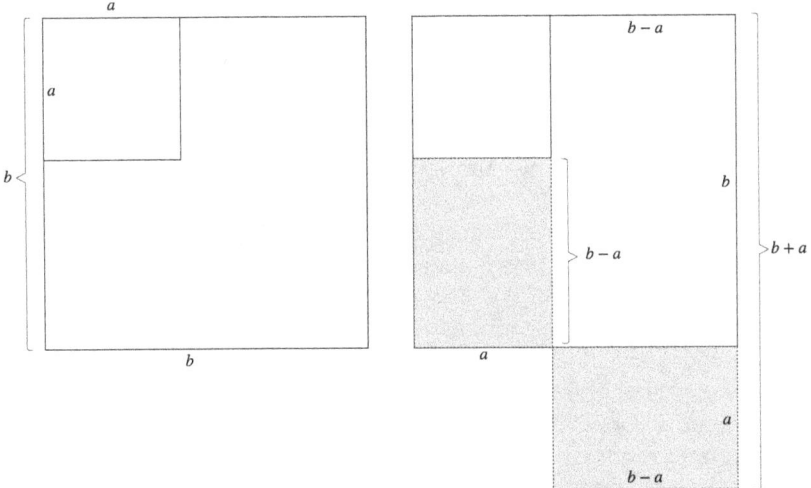

We can get more understanding by looking at a picture.

In the left part of the diagram, we see two squares, one whose side length is b (which thus has area b^2), and one nested inside it whose side length is a (and thus has area a^2). The difference of the squares, $b^2 - a^2$, is the area of the L-shaped region left behind when the a square is removed from the b square. On the right part of the diagram, we have kept the same shape but have also shaded in two rectangles. Looking at those shaded rectangles, we see that they are the same size, both of dimensions a by $(b - a)$, so they both have area $a \times (b - a)$. So the L-shaped region made up of the big white rectangle and the left grey rectangle must be the same area as the longer rectangle made up of the big white rectangle and the lower grey rectangle. But that latter, longer rectangle has dimensions $b + a$ by $b - a$, so its area is $(b + a) \times (b - a)$. This may give us a deeper understanding of the equation.

In fact, this diagram can even give us insight into the formal algebraic manipulations themselves. Notice that the big white rectangle has dimensions $b \times (b - a)$, and the smaller grey rectangle has dimensions $a \times (b - a)$. The fact that the rectangle has the same area, whether you rotate it so that the long side is horizontal or the long side is vertical, corresponds to the commutative rule, saying that $a \times (b - a) = (b - a) \times a$. Putting the rectangle on the bottom, to give us the longer rectangle, tells us that $(b + a) \times (b - a) = b \times (b - a) + a \times (b - a)$, as our first application of the distributive rule showed. The second set of applications of the distributive rule corresponds to seeing that the area of the white rectangle on the right is the area of the large square minus the left strip, and seeing that the area of the grey rectangle on the left is the left strip minus the small square. The final equation corresponds to noticing that the area of the L-shaped region is the whole square minus the left strip, plus the left strip minus the small square.

Hopefully, following this geometric explanation has helped provide some substantive insight and understanding beyond the formal symbol manipulation provided in the algebraic argument. This is by no means a full explanation—mathematicians who work on these sorts of issues in algebra and geometry will often bring in many other different areas of mathematics as well, such as number theory, set theory, topology, complex analysis, and so on, each one of which brings a different aspect of understanding to a result that can often be translated between them. We have just gotten a taste of this by looking at one result through two different branches of mathematics.

13.2   II.

Many of the important points in the story "Division by Zero" depend on the difference between mathematical insight and mechanical formalism. Renee prides herself on mostly working at the deeper level of insight, while many other mathematicians, including her department chair Peter Fabrisi, mostly work at the level of formal manipulation. Many central philosophical issues about mathematics involve this distinction, and the story alludes to many of them.

Intuitive understanding of a mathematical result is definitely more satisfying. But it's also not systematic—each piece of understanding relies on someone figuring out just what to focus on (which diagram, or which configuration of shapes, or which point) in order to get it. The formalism, instead, just provides a set of rules and a method for following them, that is guaranteed to get the answer if you work at it long enough. Math classes (particularly introductory classes whose students will go on to work on something else) often focus on the formalisms, because having a method that eventually finds the answer in all cases is more practical. But mathematicians themselves would usually rather have the insight that frames each particular result in its own unique way, rather than the ugly and unilluminating brute force method. We can think of the difference between a

Sherlock Holmes, who looks around aimlessly until he identifies the one clue that gets to the core of a case, and an insurance claims investigator who works down a checklist and eventually comes to a good enough conclusion about what must have happened.

In addition to the fact that the mechanical formalism is often systematic, it also usually both makes it easier to explain your reasoning to someone else and easier to verify that no mistake has been made. Although we like to fantasize about a Sherlock Holmes who convincingly identifies the true crux of the matter, in reality we're more comfortable with the investigator who can show us the checklist than with the wannabe Sherlock Holmes who may just have a convincing-sounding explanation that hides some hidden flaw.

We often say that something is "more of an art than a science" when there is no checklist or recipe that can be followed to do it. But this is misleading about what research scientists actually do. What we refer to in that phrase as "a science" is a recipe or checklist that anyone can learn to follow (perhaps with a few years of university study). But researchers who actually develop these "sciences" are themselves working more in the mode of "an art". Just like Renee, a cutting-edge researcher in solar energy, or viral genetics, or computer engineering, will constantly look for new and creative insights into their field that they can derive from looking at it through a new lens, from a seemingly unrelated angle, in a way that no one can anticipate. One result of this collective research process is a set of formalized methods that can be taught to many people, so that every neighborhood can have mechanics and pharmacists and IT specialists that improve our lives.

This is not to say that only a select few people have the capacity for understanding or insight—just that the formalism is what we can systematically teach—while the understanding or insight is something that people have to organically develop. It can be a joy to work with a mechanic, or a doctor, or an accountant who has deep insight into the issues you are dealing with—but it isn't necessary if you just want someone who will fix your problem and give you a set of instructions to avoid running into it again.

13.3 III.

Now we can see what goes wrong when we let a formalism float free of the rules. The following argument is alluded to at the start of section 2 of the story "Division by Zero".

Let $a = b = 1$. Since $a = 1$, multiplying both sides by a yields $a^2 = a$. Similarly, since $b = 1$, multiplying both sides by b yields $b^2 = b$. Now subtract the two sides of $a^2 = a$ from the corresponding sides of $b^2 = b$, to yield $b^2 - a^2 = b - a$. By our earlier result, $b^2 - a^2 = (b - a) \times (b + a)$, so we have $(b - a) \times (b + a) = b - a$. Dividing both sides by $b - a$, we get that $b + a = 1$. But this means that $1 + 1 = 1$! Looking through more carefully, and plugging in the values $a = b = 1$, we can verify that every equation in our reasoning was correct, even up to $(b - a) \times (b + a) = b - a$. $((1 - 1) \times (1 + 1)$ is in fact 0×2, which does in fact equal $1 - 1$.) It only went wrong in the last step, when we divided by $b - a$, which meant that we were dividing by zero.

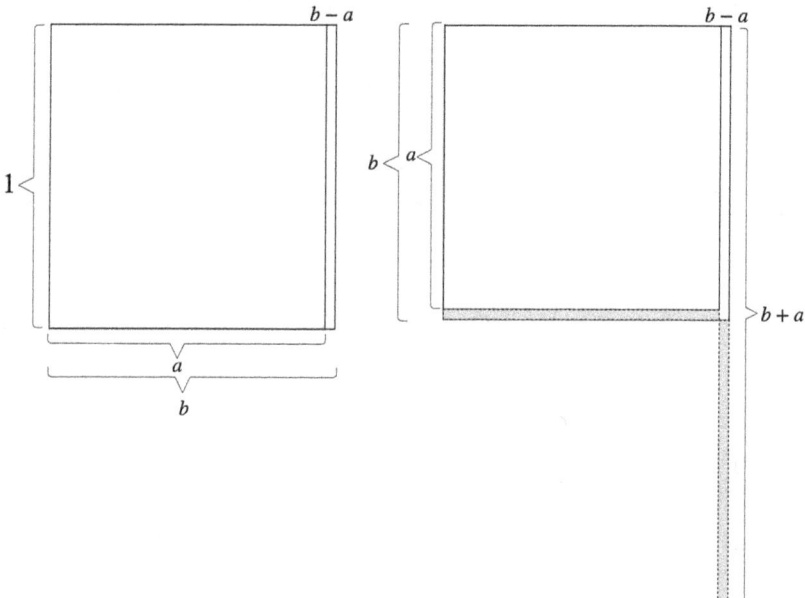

When we try to draw this out in a diagram, we can see what goes wrong.

This is what the diagram would look like if a and b were both very close to 1. On the left, we have rectangles of height 1, and width a and b, respectively. On the right, we have two nested squares, with side length a and b, respectively. When we claim that multiplying both sides of the equation $a = 1$ by a yields a new equation, $a^2 = a$, we are claiming that the square of side a on the right has the same area as the $a \times 1$ rectangle on the left. Similarly, the equation $b^2 = b$ claims that the square of side b on the right has the same area as the $b \times 1$ rectangle on the left. When we take the differences, we claim that the vertical sliver between the rectangles on the left has the same area as the L-shaped sliver between the squares on the right—which is the same as the area of the tall rectangle on the right. Since the two rectangles both have the width of $b - a$, we then claim that their height must be the same, so $1 = b + a$. We can see that when $a \neq b$ none of the steps in this reasoning are right—but when $a = b$ everything is in fact precisely right, even including the point where we say the two rectangles have the same area. But the reason they have the same area is that they both have area 0. Dividing by 0 corresponds to claiming that two rectangles with the same area and the same width must have the same height—which is true, as long as the width is not 0.

As the story says, the standard response is just to note that division by zero is not allowed—you break the formalism by doing that. But it is hard to notice this rule every time it matters—and some important parts of mathematical history are built on breaking it.

The central question of the mathematical subject we now know as "calculus" is about measuring the slope, not of a line, but of a general curve. Isaac Newton had an idea of how to do this, during the plague year of 1665 when he had to stay home from university. If we want to measure the slope of a curve that is given by some mathematical function, say, the parabola given by $f(x) = x^2$, we can approximate the slope at a point by finding two points near it and calculating the slope between them.

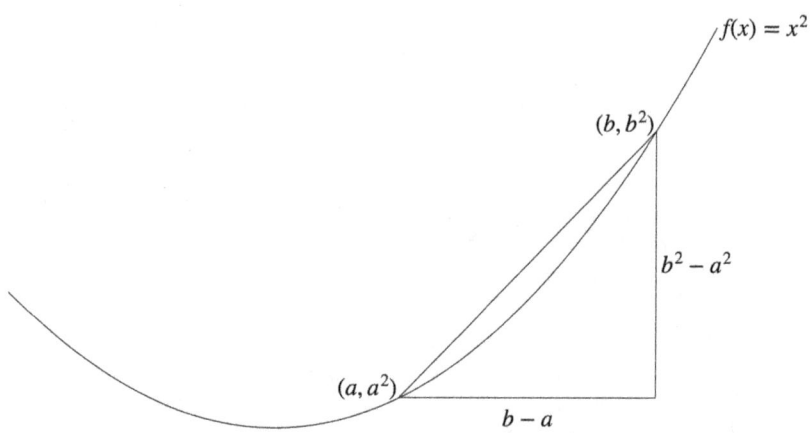

So, for instance, we can consider two points on this curve, (a, a^2) and (b, b^2), and calculate the slope of the line connecting them. The vertical separation between the two points is $b^2 - a^2$, and the horizontal separation is $b - a$, so the slope of this line is $\frac{b^2 - a^2}{b-a}$. As we have noted several times, $b^2 - a^2 = (b-a)(b+a)$, so when we divide by $b-a$, we get that this slope is $b + a$. Newton notes that when a and b are distinct numbers, we get the slope connecting two different points on the curve, which isn't quite what we want—so we should just let b and a be the *same* number if we want to calculate the slope of the curve *precisely* at that point. At the point (a, a^2), he says, the slope of the curve $f(x) = x^2$ is precisely $2a$. He did similar things to compute the slopes of other curves and put this together with his new theory of gravity to discover the shape of the solar system, and his method was central to all of physics for the next several centuries.

But, did you notice? He divided by $b - a$, and then said that $b = a$, so he was dividing by zero. The philosopher (and Bishop of the Anglican Church of Ireland) George Berkeley noticed and wrote a treatise in 1734 attacking Newton for this (though not by name, since by then Newton was too well-respected by contemporaries for even a luminary of the church to go after). Just as atheists ridiculed the church for teaching that one and the same God is sometimes the father, sometimes the son, and sometimes the holy ghost, Berkeley ridiculed the "infidel mathematician" for teaching that $b - a$ is sometimes non-zero, when you divide by it, and sometimes zero, when you calculate at the end, and must thus be just the "ghost of a departed quantity".

Since Newton's formal tools for calculation worked and didn't seem to lead to contradiction, most mathematicians just ignored Berkeley and went on doing what they were doing. But by the early nineteenth century, contradictions were building up. Leonhard Euler had extended Newton's methods to compute various infinite sums and solved some long-standing problems—but also ended up with strange claims like $1 + 2 + 3 + \ldots = -1/12$. Augustin Cauchy used Newton's methods to "prove" that a certain construction always yields a continuous function—but Joseph Fourier showed how to construct the discontinuous sawtooth wave in this way. Giovanni Saccheri "proved" that Euclid's parallel postulate followed from the others—but Bernhard Riemann showed that it was possible to reject the parallel postulate without trouble.

By the late nineteenth century, these errors were being fixed. Karl Weierstrass had developed a new formalism to justify Newton's calculations that avoided division by zero, and he and others separated Euler's truths from his mistakes and showed where Cauchy and Saccheri had gone wrong. This set the stage in 1900 for David Hilbert to propose, as one of the most important open problems for mathematics the challenge of finding a formalism that would work for all of mathematics and prove that it is consistent. The introductions to many of the numbered sections of the story refer to key moments in this project—Russell and Whitehead's *Principia Mathematica*, which was a formalism sufficient to encompass all the mathematics of the time, Gödel's proof that only a stronger system could ever prove this system consistent, Gentzen's construction of such a stronger system.

13.4 IV.

If Hilbert's program had succeeded, then mathematics would have been consistent—but reduced to a formal system. The invention of computers would have meant that mathematics no longer existed as a field of research. There would be no more reason for the mathematics that is "more of an art than a science". But it would have been sound. The philosopher Imre Lakatos argued (1978) that early calculus mostly avoided contradiction because of the understanding that early mathematicians had, even though their formalism was unsound. But Hilbert's dream was a sound formalism that would have made understanding unnecessary.

Gödel, like many other mathematicians and philosophers since then, saw his results as preserving the importance of creativity and understanding in mathematics. But people whose lives depend on our ability to solve difficult mathematical problems (which is increasingly all of us, as mathematics becomes more central to biology, banking, ballistics, and everything else) may have wanted there to be a way to automate mathematics and let humans pursue creativity and understanding in music or poetry instead. Even despite the fact that there can be no universal computer system for mathematics, some mathematicians have argued in recent decades that it is important enough to get things right that we should start producing proofs that can be verified by computers, rather than proofs that humans can use for their own purposes. I have said more about why I think mathematicians generally reject this movement in two of my previous publications (Easwaran 2009, 2015).

The story of "Division by Zero" explores the opposite catastrophe and reaches a surprisingly similar conclusion, where there is nothing left of interest in mathematics. When mathematical understanding inevitably leads to contradiction, all that is left is meaningless symbol manipulation. This is often what many people assume that mathematics is, when they haven't experienced the understanding for themselves. But mathematicians themselves have always sought understanding and used symbols only as a way to keep their expressions more precise for communication.

References

Easwaran, K. 2009. Probabilistic Proofs and Transferability. *Philosophia Mathematica* 17 (3): 341–362.

———. 2015. Rebutting and Undercutting in Mathematics. *Philosophical Perspectives* 29:146–162.

Lakatos, I. 1978. Cauchy and the Continuum. *The Mathematical Intelligencer* 1 (3): 151–161.

CHAPTER 14

Choosing What's Fictionally True

Hannah H. Kim

14.1 Introduction

Fictional truth may sound like an oxymoron, but it's not. Fictional truth is what we take to be true in, or according to, a fictional story. It is fictionally true that Cathy Ames runs away from her parents (in and according to *East of Eden*), and it is fictionally true that Ifemelu runs a popular blog (in and according to *Americanah*).

Are there any limits to what can be fictionally true? It is intuitive to think that there is no limit to what can be true in a fiction, and that fiction is different from nonfiction precisely because "anything goes" when it comes to fiction. However, some philosophers question this sentiment.

One might think that moral truths—like "murder is morally bad"—are necessary truths, meaning there is no way for "murder is morally bad" to *not* be true. If moral truths are necessary truths, then not even a fictional story can create a scenario where murder isn't morally bad.

Logical truths or mathematical truths might also be thought of as necessary. Some philosophers argue that not even a made-up story can violate the law of identity—that each thing is identical to itself—or the law of

H. H. Kim (✉)
Tucson, AZ, USA
e-mail: hhkim@arizona.edu

noncontradiction—that no sentence is both true and false. If they're right, then no one could write a story where a character is and isn't a professor or tell a story where James Bond somehow is not identical to James Bond.

When engaging with fictional stories, why do we have trouble imagining certain morally deviant claims or logically contradictory claims? One explanation is that we simply cannot imagine there being morally good female infanticide or a five-fingered oval. This is the *cantian* analysis of the phenomena since the fact that we can't imagine certain things is what supposedly produces imaginative resistance. Another explanation appeals to the fact that we can but sometimes refuse to imagine certain things to be true in a fiction; perhaps we won't entertain, even for the sake of reading, a world where it's good to kill a baby girl. This is the *wontian* analysis of imaginative resistance (see Tuna 2020 for an overview of imaginative resistance).

In "Division by Zero", Renée Norwood is described to have proven that 1=2. But is it possible for someone to formulate a proof that 1=2? To prove that 1=2 is to prove that math is inconsistent.

I mentioned that mathematical truths might be *necessary* truths, meaning that there is no way for mathematical truths to be otherwise. This is a widely held view. Once we fix the meaning of "1", "=", and "2", 1=2 is false, and necessarily false, meaning there is no possibility that 1=2 is true. So, what Renée pulls off in the story is a mathematical impossibility.

We might be tempted to think that what Renée does is possible given the story's appeal to Kurt Gödel's incompleteness theorems (the second of which says a consistent mathematical system based on axioms cannot prove its own consistency with those axioms) and the narrator's claim from chapter 6 that "arithmetic as a formal system cannot guarantee that it will not produce results such as '1 = 2'". However, the inability to "guarantee"—or prove—something doesn't show the contrast to be possible. I can't prove from the axioms of arithmetic that I'm not identical to my sister, but that doesn't make it possible that I am her! Gödel's second theorem isn't about the consistency of mathematical systems *per se*; it implies instead that such systems can't prove or ground their own consistency. Our intuitions and inference to the best explanation suggest arithmetic is indeed consistent (1 *just doesn't* equal 2! And why would math be so effective if not consistent?). And if arithmetic is consistent, it is necessarily consistent even if it can't prove its own consistency—so what Renée does is like squaring the circle: seemingly meaningful but impossible.

So, it's no surprise that some readers I've talked to don't take it to be fictionally true that Renée proves arithmetic to be inconsistent. They merely take it to be fictionally true that she *believes* that she proved 1=2. Those who don't want to—or can't—imagine something that is impossible have a reason to think that Renée couldn't have actually proven 1=2 since mathematical truths are necessarily true, i.e., true everywhere, at all times.

I happen to think that impossible things can be true according to a work of fiction.[1] But setting my own convictions aside, and given the available cantian and wontian explanations of why some readers resist Renée's accomplishment, how should we analyze what is fictionally true in "Division by Zero"? The above considerations represent philosophical attempts to begin with beliefs about the nature of possibility and imagination to guide us in determining what can and can't be fictionally true. In the rest of the chapter, I'll see what happens once we compare the aesthetic or artistic merits of taking the story at face value (and admit that Renée in the story does prove 1=2) with a reading that considers Renée to have been mistaken. This method highlights the aesthetic costs of thinking that certain things can't be fictionally true, which gives us a new starting point on how we ought to decide what is and isn't a limit to fictional truth.

14.2 A Reading of the Story Where Renée Proves 1=2

Renée and Carl are married, and "Division by Zero" weaves three narrative strands together. The numbered chapters tell the story of mathematics; "A" chapters are about Renée or told from her perspective; "B" chapters are about Carl or told from his perspective. The way these chapters are presented is worth a close look because their connections change as the story unfolds.

Chapters 1A and 1B cover the same stretch of time—Renée being released from the hospital—but from the respective perspectives of Renée and Carl. Chapters 2A and 2B also cover the same portion of time—they are now home from the hospital—but this time, we encounter memories of each character. We also get foreshadowing; in 2B, Carl finds nothing wrong in the way he supported Renée, just as she will find nothing wrong

---

[1] See Xhignesse (2016, 2020, 2021) and Kim (forthcoming) for aesthetic and cognitive considerations that bear on what can and can't be fictionally true.

in her proof in 4A. Chapters 3A and 3B are functionally parallel in that they both provide an account of how Renée and Carl became the people they are. We meet Renée at age seven when her interest in math is born, and we meet Carl in grad school as he recovers from a suicide attempt and learns how to empathize. Chapter 4 tells the story of math trying to get on surer footing, and in chapter 4A Renée first becomes puzzled with her new proof that 1=2. This is the first time the A chapter and B chapter timelines intersect as we learn about how Renée and Carl met. Chapters 5A and 5B separate as they both struggle to understand: Renée can't understand how her proof can be free of error; Carl doesn't understand why Renée feels and acts the way she does.

Then we get the first true continuity between timelines, meaning 6B picks up where 6A left off. Why is this? One possible clue is that chapter 6 introduces Gödel's incompleteness theorems, which suggests that we can't guarantee we won't encounter the kind of contradictions that Renée proves. Perhaps Renée and Carl's stories line up once we realize the possibility of a contradiction—or something thought to be impossible—being shown as true. This sense of continuity further develops in chapters 7A and 7B as Renée and Carl's respective intuitions lead them both to detrimental results. Renée's theorem *feels right* to her; Carl realizes that he can't feel anything for Renée. Chapter 8 asks "what now?" Hilbert's question—"If mathematical thinking is defective, where are we to find truth and certitude?"—suggests that truth in general is in jeopardy if we consider mathematical thinking defective. For Renée, math is no longer of interest to her since it is now empirical, meaningless and inconsistent once it goes beyond physical entities. For Carl, the breakdown of empathy makes him question what, if anything, is fundamental to who he is.

Finally, the story ends on a formally significant note as chapter 9—the final story of math—relays a quote from Einstein saying we can't have certainty *and* real-world connection in math and chapters 9A and 9B are equated to each other. 9A=B is an explicit invitation for us to compare "A" and "B", Renée and Carl. The comparison is apt since what Renée and Carl go through are structurally identical—but there's also something impossible about the equation since, after all, Renée *isn't* Carl. Similarly, the story ends with a seeming emotional impossibility since Carl feels an empathy that separates him from Renée. An "empathy that separates" feels like a contradiction, just as proof that 1=2 feels like a contradiction.

We can pull out several themes from the above observations. The first thing to note is the parallel experience between Renée and Carl. As the integrity of math breaks down for her, the marriage breaks down for him. The significance of the title becomes clear here as both Renée and Carl must chart unknown territory after their respective realizations. Dividing by zero destabilizes the future since no more rules apply, and we see how new knowledge threatens the two individuals' understanding of themselves and the world. The new learnings are like division by zero, "forbidden," something after which nothing makes sense anymore. The final 9A=B chapter is powerful because there really is an equivalence of experience.

Another noteworthy feature is the nonlinear form of the story. If all numbers are equal, perhaps there is no meaningful difference between a story narrated "in order" and a story narrated "out of order"—so the fact that the story jumps around in time is a mirrored response to the content that Renée comes to prove. The story also begins and ends with the same gesture from Renée (looking out the window). Why come back to where things started? Perhaps the return to the beginning suggests a kind of wholeness, or a kind of sense, that can still be had even when there is an impossibility involved. There's also a mirroring going on between the couple. Seeing things like Carl (empirically) upsets Renée, and experiencing what Renée is going through (having a foundational belief undermined) upsets Carl.

Finally, the story gestures to figures and objects outside of the story. Given Renée's desire for *a priori* knowledge—knowledge that isn't empirical but known without experience—makes one wonder if she is named after Descartes, just as Carl's emotional sensitivity makes one wonder whether he is named after Jung or Rogers. The story also has thematic connections to Ted Chiang's "What's Expected of Us" in its poignant contrast between (merely, theoretically) understanding something and (fully, genuinely) grasping something. Many mathematicians are unbothered by Renée's proof just as most people are unbothered by the Predictor in "What's Expected of Us", a machine that always "knows" when a person is about to press a button and thereby demonstrates the lack of free will. However, those who truly grasp, and not just understand, the implications of the Predictor lose the ability to go on as before, as Renée does.

14.3 What Is Lost in a Reading Where Renée Doesn't In Fact Prove 1=2

Recall the various reasons someone might prefer an interpretation of "Division by Zero" where Renée merely believes that she proves arithmetic to be inconsistent without in fact doing so. One might not want to commit to a mathematical impossibility to be true even in fiction. Or one might have difficulties robustly imagining that 1=2. What, if anything, is lost in this more restrictive interpretation that bars a mathematical impossibility from being fictionally true?

First, the narration would lose credibility. Renée is repeatedly presented as a talented mathematician, but if she is mistaken about her proof, a reader would need to temper her estimation of Renée's intellectual capacity. Renée is presented as a knower even in domains that have nothing to do with math—she knows what to say at the psychiatric hospital to feign wellness and knows what her colleague or husband will say—so we might need to adjust our understanding of her more broadly. Perhaps she's more of a know-it-all than a person who genuinely knows many things.

Going this route takes on the burden of explaining away evidence we're offered to take Renée's feat at face value. She explicitly rejects the possibility that she's mistaken (though, to be fair, anyone who is mistaken would say the same thing). More convincing are the facts that she arrives at the same contradictory conclusion in more than one way, that she's never found math difficult, and that the mistake is sophisticated enough to survive the mathematical community's scrutiny.

Finally, many of the thematic patterns that we identified in the last section become weak or irrelevant if Renée is mistaken. The parallel developments of Carl and Renée were predicated on the fact that Carl considered empathy to be a fundamental aspect of himself and found that to be false *and* that Renée considered arithmetic to be fundamentally consistent and found that to be false. Another parallel had to do with the couple's commitment to knowledge: Carl continually strove to learn about Renée's emotional life and came to really know her and her tendencies. For Renée to mirror this aspect of Carl, she would also have to really know things about math. If Carl was correct in his assessment, and Renée mistaken in hers, then the strength of the parallel wanes. The overall point isn't that the parallels go away entirely if we were to say that it's Carl and Renée's mere beliefs that are shown to be wrong, but that the force and significance of the parallels decrease, which affects the story's poignancy.

These disruptions to the mirroring between Carl and Renée diminish the significance of 9A=9B. "A" and "B" don't quite line up as neatly, so the final chapter becomes cheeky at best. Accordingly, the choice to narrate in a nonlinear fashion becomes less a formal ramification of arithmetic's inconsistency, and the story's thematic connection to "What's Expected of Us" also breaks down since the stories no longer mutually highlight the difference between mere understanding and genuine grasping/intuiting—Renée neither understands nor intuits according to this second reading! Finally, an interpretation that takes Renée to be mistaken doesn't comport as well with Chiang's story notes where he says "[a] proof that mathematics is inconsistent, and that all its wonderous beauty was just an illusion, would, it seems to me, be one of the worst things you could ever learn". If the story was meant to be a working out of this idea, the natural interpretation of "Division by Zero" would be that a character genuinely proves, and learns, math to be inconsistent, and not that she mistakenly believes to have done so.

Of course, none of the considerations in this section make it definitive that Renée's proof was correct. But I hope to have shown that the aesthetic costs of this alternative interpretation are high. In short, the story is better if we interpret it so that Renée really does prove that 1=2.

14.4 Conclusion

"Division by Zero" is a case study that lets us weigh the aesthetic costs of approaching fiction with metaphysical commitments insisting that fictional truth be consistent or possible. In this particular case, I believe the costs outweigh the benefits. Many of the features that make the story aesthetically good are lost once we refuse to acknowledge that Renée really proves arithmetic to be inconsistent.

Ultimately, I think we have a choice in where we start. Will we choose our theoretical commitments about fiction first and face whatever aesthetic consequences there are? Or will we consider the aesthetic features of a work and then adopt metaphysical requirements that support those features? (Of course, these decisions will be made in equilibrium since we need to start with *some* metaphysical commitments to even begin to acknowledge fiction as fiction.) My only plea is that we not always prioritize the metaphysics first, especially if we want to develop the kinds of theories of fiction and fictional truth that track the way most people engage with fiction.

Acknowledgments I'd like to thank Mark Balaguer, Kenny Easwaran, and David Friedell for helpful discussions and feedback on a previous draft.

References

Kim, Hannah H. forthcoming. Imagination and the Permissive View of Fictional Truth. *The Australasian Journal of Philosophy*.

Tuna, Emine Hande. 2020. Imaginative Resistance. In *The Stanford Encyclopedia of Philosophy* (Summer 2020 Edition), ed. Edward N. Zalta. https://plato.stanford.edu/archives/sum2020/entries/imaginative-resistance/. Accessed 28 November 2023.

Xhignesse, Michel-Antoine. 2016. The Trouble with Poetic License. *British Journal of Aesthetics* 56 (2): 149–161.

———. 2020. Exploding Stories and the Limits of Fiction. *Philosophical Studies* 178:675–692.

———. 2021. Imagining Fictional Contradictions. *Synthese* 99:3169–3188.

PART VIII

Time

CHAPTER 15

Time Machines and Predictors are Possible but Unlikely

David Friedell

The concept of time is prevalent in Ted Chiang's writing. In "The Merchant and The Alchemist's Gate", Fuwaad and other characters travel back and forth in time through the Gate of Years. In "What's Expected of Us", a device called a Predictor always flashes green a second *before* someone presses its button. And, in "Story of Your Life", Louise and the Heptapods experience the past, present, and future all at once.

These stories beautifully demonstrate that both time travel and infallibly predicting the future are possible. But, if, like me, you'd love to have a time machine or a Predictor, don't get your hopes up. With just a little philosophy, we can see that these technologies, though possible, are unlikely to ever exist. No engineering or physics required.

15.1 Why Time Machines Are Possible

The word *possible* is tricky. Sometimes when we say something is possible we mean it's consistent with current technology. Self-driving cars are technologically possible, but flying cars are not (yet). Sometimes when we say

D. Friedell (✉)
Philosophy, Union College, Schenectady, NY, USA
e-mail: friedeld@union.edu

© The Author(s), under exclusive license to Springer Nature Switzerland AG 2025
D. Friedell (ed.), *The Philosophy of Ted Chiang*,
https://doi.org/10.1007/978-3-031-81662-8_15

something is possible we mean it's consistent with the laws of physics. It's physically possible (though extremely unlikely) for me to run faster than Usain Bolt. But it's physically *im*possible for anyone to run faster than the speed of light. When I say that time machines and Predictors are possible, I'm not talking about technological or physical possibility. I'm talking about something much broader, which philosophers sometimes call *metaphysical* possibility.

Almost everything is possible in this very broad sense. It's metaphysically possible for there to be flying cars. It's even metaphysically possible to run faster than the speed of light. As the great sage and power forward Kevin Garnett once said: "Anything is possible!" More precisely, *almost* anything is possible. The main exception is this: contradictions are impossible. A contradiction is a situation in which a sentence is both true and false. For example, it's contradictory to say both that I am in Portugal and that I'm not in Portugal. It's possible for me to be in Portugal. It's possible for me to *not* be in Portugal. But it's not possible—metaphysically—for me to both be in Portugal and not be in Portugal at the same time. That's a contradiction.

So, when I say that time machines and Predictors are possible, what I mean is that both of those technologies could exist without anything contradictory happening. How do I know this? Well, for one thing, Ted Chiang has written entertaining stories about these technologies with no contradictions. This is no small feat. Many time travel stories and many stories about infallible predictors (or oracles) contain contradictions. Consider this very short and very cliché time travel story.

Changing the Past
Eighty years after the Holocaust, a scientist builds a time machine. She travels back in time and kills Hitler when he is a baby. As a result, the Holocaust never happens.

Can you spot the contradiction? The first sentence contradicts the last sentence. The first sentence says the Holocaust happened and the last sentence says it never happened. An event can't both happen and not happen; that's a contradiction. So, this story is not only cliché. It's impossible.

In fact, any story about someone changing the past is contradictory and thus impossible. This happens in a lot of stories. Let's take a famous example: the movie *Back to the Future*. It's initially true in the movie that a car hit Marty McFly's dad in 1955, which led to Marty's parents falling in love. Marty then travels in a time machine from 1985 to 1955 and pushes his dad out of the way so that the car does not hit his dad. The car hits Marty instead, Marty's mom becomes enamored with Marty, and hijinks ensue. This is a contradiction. Either the car hit Marty's dad, or it did not. It's impossible for it to be true that the car hit Marty's dad *and* that it did not. The number one rule of time travel is this: you can't change the past. It's impossible to change the past, because doing so would create a contradiction. Don't get me wrong. I'm not a snob. I love the movie. It's just contradictory and thus impossible.

But, and this is a subtle point, even though it's impossible to *change* the past, it's still possible for a time traveler to *affect* the past. Ted Chiang's "The Merchant and the Alchemist's Gate" illustrates this difference between changing and affecting the past. Raniya, the wife of the wealthy merchant Hassan, enters the Gate of Years and travels to Cairo twenty years in the past. There she enacts a clever scheme (with the help of her older time traveling self) that prevents Hassan from being killed by bandits. After saving Hassan's life, Raniya instructs him "in the art of love", without him knowing that one day he will marry her. Note that Raniya is *not* an invisible time traveler who quietly observes but does not affect the past. She affects it vividly, both in saving Hassan's life and in sleeping with him. But—and this is the key point—in doing so she does not *change* the past. There is only one timeline, and it is one in which Raniya "always" saves Hassan's life, and then they subsequently sleep with each other. There's no alternative timeline where these events don't occur.

Even though it's impossible to change the past, there's nothing to stop a time traveler from trying. In "The Merchant and the Alchemist's Gate", Fuwaad knows that his wife died twenty years ago in a horrific accident. He travels from Baghdad to Cairo, enters the Gate of Years, travels twenty years back to the past, and then travels back to Baghdad to try to save his wife. Due to a string of unfortunate events, including a sandstorm, he gets there too late, just a day after she died. This is unfortunate, but not impossible. Since Fuwaad fails to change the past, there's no contradiction. His journey, though unsuccessful in some respects, is still invaluable. Shortly after Fuwaad discovers that he has arrived too late, a nurse who was with his wife when she died passes along a loving message to him. This illustrates how, although the past is unchangeable, time travelers may affect and be affected by the past. Fuwaad is *affected* by the past—his wife's message deeply moves him.

So, nothing contradictory happens in "The Merchant and the Alchemist's Gate". Strange things still occur. One of the strangest things enables Hassan to be wealthy. Hassan as a younger, poorer man enters the Gate of Years to go twenty years in the future. There his older, wealthier self tells him where to find buried treasure in the desert. He goes back twenty years into the past and finds the treasure. How did the older Hassan know the treasure's location? Well, he learned it when he was twenty years younger from his then older self in the way I just described. If you stop and think about this, it's strange. Really strange. Younger Hassan learns the treasure's location from Older Hassan, who in turn learned it from Older Hassan when he was younger. But what explains how "they" know the treasure's location in the first place? There's no explanation. Or, as Older Hassan says, "there's no explanation except that it was the will of Allah, and what other explanation is there for anything?"

Philosophers call these scenarios *causal loops*. An earlier event causes a later event, which in turn causes the earlier event, which in turn causes the later event, and so forth. Although each event in the loop has an explanation there's no explanation for why the entire loop exists (other than perhaps Allah's will). As David Lewis explains, these causal loops are strange but they're not impossible.[1] It's strange for something to happen without a bigger explanation, but it's totally possible. There's no *contradiction* in Hassan learning the treasure's location from his older self, aging twenty years, then telling his younger self the treasure's location. It's just strange. But I never claimed time travel would be ordinary. Just that it's possible.

Ted Chiang is not the only author to tell a strange yet possible time travel story without any contradictions. Robert Heinlen's "All You Zombies" and Audrey Niffenegger's *The Time Traveller's Wife* are two of my favorites in this genre. But few authors tell possible time travel stories that are as moving and as memorable as Chiang's "The Merchant and the Alchemist's Gate".

15.2 Why Predictors Are Possible

Just as "The Merchant and the Alchemist's Gate" illustrates how time travel is possible, Chiang's "What's Expected of Us" illustrates how infallible predictors are possible. Infallible predictors, unlike meteorologists, make only accurate predictions. Many different kinds of things could be

---

[1] This entire section is heavily influenced by Lewis's classic paper "The Paradoxes of Time Travel" (1976). It's my bible on the subject.

infallible predictors: an all-knowing god, an oracle, or, as in "What's Expected of Us", a Predictor.

Predictors have a button that, when pressed, sends a signal a second into the past that causes a green light on the device to flash. So, if you have a Predictor that is flashing green you *know* you will press its button a second from now. Likewise, if your Predictor isn't flashing green you *know* you will *not* press its button a second from now. In this way, Predictors make only accurate predictions. Granted, their power is limited. They can't tell you how the stock market will do or even what the weather will be. But they tell you with absolute certainty whether or not you will press a button a second into the future. That's still pretty cool, and I would want one.

Maybe you wouldn't want one, because you worry a Predictor would reveal you don't have free will and cause you extreme distress. That's how many people in the story respond. I agree with Mark Balaguer who argues in this volume that extreme distress would be a gross overreaction. Let us set aside the question of whether Predictors are *desirable* (as I think they are) and focus instead on whether they are *possible*.

In order to appreciate that Predictors are possible we need only remind ourselves that there's a big difference between saying something is strange and saying that it's impossible. Whenever a Predictor flashes green the person using it presses its button a second later. Whenever the light is not on the person will not press its button a second later. There's no exception to these rules. An exception would cause a contradiction, given the story's stipulation that Predictors are infallible. But since there's no exception nothing contradictory happens. Infallible predictors are strange but not impossible. Of course, I'm not claiming these devices are technologically or physically possible. I'm merely claiming that they are metaphysically possible.

Chiang's writing provides an example of another infallible predictor: Fuwaad himself. Fuwaad convinces a guard he is from the future by predicting that a governor's son will be born with albinism. Soon after, that prediction comes true. Fuwaad is confident in his prediction, because he is from the future and remembers it happening. "The Merchant and the Alchemist's Gate" ends with Fuwaad offering his predictive powers to the Caliph of Baghdad. Assuming that there's nothing wrong with Fuwaad's memory, he is an infallible predictor. His predictions will come true, because, just as there's no way to change the past, there's no way to change the future. Doing so would cause a contradiction.

15.3 Why Time Machines and Predictors Are Unlikely

Even though time machines and Predictors are possible, I'm convinced they are unlikely to ever exist. This is due to an argument about time travel originated by Paul Horwich and defended more recently by Katrina Elliott.[2]

Here's the basic idea. Suppose people were to have time machines. What would happen? Some people would go to the past to witness some famous historical event, maybe a concert or something like that. Many others, however, like Fuwaad, would try to change the past. It's very natural to *try* to change the past. Fuwaad is convinced he cannot change the past, but still can't help but try. I'd probably do the same. It's human nature.

No time traveler, however, would successfully change the past. Because doing so, as we've seen, is impossible. So, *something* would stop them from changing the past. In Fuwaad's case there's a string of unfortunate events, including a sandstorm. Fuwaad is unlucky but not uniquely so. Any time traveler who tries to prevent a loved one who died in the past from dying will fail. They'll have a sudden heart attack, or their mode of transportation will fail them, or they'll slip on a banana peel at the most inopportune time, or something of that sort. Even if thousands and thousands of time travelers try, they will all fail, just as Fuwaad failed. For each time traveler there will be a coincidence, or, as in the case of Fuwaad, a string of coincidences that will thwart their plans.

We can now see why time travel is unlikely. If time machines were ever available, many people would try to change the past. They would all fail, due to unlikely occurrences. But so many unlikely things happening is, well, unlikely. So, it's unlikely that time travel will ever occur. That's Horwich's argument in a nutshell.

This argument doesn't say time travel is impossible. Just that it's unlikely. It's possible that if I flip a fair coin it will come up heads 100 times in a row. It's just extremely unlikely. It's also possible that I will make 100 free throws in a row next time I go to a basketball court. That's also extremely unlikely. We know that time travel is unlikely, because we know that time travelers will consistently fail at things that are very easy to do. It's possible for people to fail at things that are easy to do. Indeed, it happens occasionally. I can be a bit of a klutz and fail to do some easy

---

[2] Paul Horwich (1987) and Katrina Elliott (2019).

things, like walk across the room without tripping. But it's unlikely I will fail to walk across the room without tripping most of the time or every time I try. And yet time travelers, if there were any, would fail at a ton of very easy things many, many times. So, time travel is unlikely.

We can extend this reasoning about time travel being unlikely to see that infallible prediction is unlikely. If a Predictor's light flashed green, I would try *not* to press its button for a whole second. It's human nature. Similarly, if its light were not flashing green, I'd try to "beat" the machine by pressing its button within a second. That, too, is human nature. But, no matter how hard I try, I would fail every single time to outwit the device. Some coincidence would cause me to press the button every time I would try to refrain—a gust of wind, a friend pushing me, a spasm. Conversely, something unlikely would prevent me from pressing the button every time I would try to press it—a sudden distraction or change of heart. I'm not unique. Many people with Predictors would fail in similarly unlikely fashion. Since such extensive failure is unlikely, Predictors are unlikely.

And here's the really strange thing. I haven't said anything sophisticated about physics or engineering. Unlike Ted Chiang, I know very little about physics or engineering. I'm just a humble country philosopher. You might have thought that in order to know whether time machines or Predictors are likely to ever exist, you should consult a physicist or engineer. But I've relied on very basic facts about human psychology, about whether time travelers would try to change the past or whether people with Predictors would try to "beat" the machine. I've relied also on very basic evidence about how easy it is to do things like travel from Cairo to Baghdad when you've got plenty of time and means, or just refrain from pressing a button for a whole second. No physics. No engineering. And yet I can't see any flaw with this argument for time travel and infallible prediction being unlikely. So, although I'd love to have a time machine or a Predictor—and I'm convinced they're possible—I won't hold my breath.

Acknowledgments Thanks to Mark Balaguer, Patrick Grafton-Cardwell, and Bradley Rettler for helpful discussion.

References

Elliott, Katrina. 2019. How to Know that Time Travel is Unlikely Without Knowing Why. *Pacific Philosophical Quarterly* 100 (1): 90–113.

Horwich, Paul. 1987. *Asymmetries in Time: Problems in the Philosophy of Science*. MIT Press.

Lewis, David. 1976. The Paradoxes of Time Travel. *American Philosophical Quarterly* 13 (2): 145–152.

CHAPTER 16

The Temporality of Our Emotions and Time in Ted Chiang's Stories

Rebecca Chan

A merchant resents himself for speaking harshly to his wife when she tells him what he already knows deep down: that his business is immoral. A mother sees her child and experiences overwhelming love and joy. Both feel the deep, consuming grief that accompanies the death of one's beloved.

Ted Chiang vividly captures these emotions in "The Merchant and the Alchemist's Gate" and "Story of Your Life." Fuwaad ibn Abbas and Louise Banks's stories resonate with us because these emotions touch us, too. Yet, Chiang's temporal construction of these stories introduces an alien element: *when* these characters experience their emotions. Because she ceases to experience time linearly, Louise sees the entirety of her daughter's life unfold all at once. She experiences joy and grief in response to her daughter's life and death *before her daughter is even born*. In Fuwaad's case, his journey back in time places his grief in the peculiar position of occurring both *prior to* and *20 years after* news of his wife's death.

R. Chan (✉)
San José State University, San Jose, CA, USA
e-mail: rebecca.s.chan@sjsu.edu

© The Author(s), under exclusive license to Springer Nature Switzerland AG 2025
D. Friedell (ed.), *The Philosophy of Ted Chiang*,
https://doi.org/10.1007/978-3-031-81662-8_16

In good science fiction, the most fantastic elements of a story force us to reimagine and reexamine common experiences—say, the temporal nature of our emotions. Here, the peculiar timing of Fuwaad and Louise's emotions reveals a puzzle about the temporality of our own emotions:[1]

1. Our emotional responses to events can be reasonable or unreasonable.
2. Once they occur, the events to which our emotions respond are permanently a part of the world, though, typically, our emotions are impermanent.
3. The change in emotions doesn't result from a change in the events to which they respond, yet the change seems reasonable.

To appreciate the tension in these three claims, take grief, the all too familiar emotion shared by Fuwaad and Louise. Grief is *reasonable* when it is an appropriate response to a tragic event, such as the loss of a loved one. Lacking the appropriate amount of grief—think of Camus's Mersault at his mother's funeral—indicates that something has gone awry. Yet, our emotions change over time, even though the underlying events do not. Typically, grief eventually subsides, even though our loved ones are not restored to us. This change in emotions seems reasonable, even though the underlying events have not changed. We're thus presented with a puzzle: what could explain the reasonableness of the temporality of our emotions?

All three of these claims seem compelling! But it also looks like they can't all be true. Explaining which is false is surprisingly challenging. To see why, let's examine each claim more closely with help from Chiang's stories.

16.1 Are Emotions Reasonable?

One response to this puzzle denies (1), which claims that emotions can be reasonable or unreasonable. This response is tempting. After all, emotions are just things that we *feel*. Often, they lie outside of our rational control, and it doesn't seem quite right to criticize people's feelings as being

---

[1] This is a simplified version of the puzzle Barislov Marušić extensively treats in *The Temporality of Emotions* (2022).

unreasonable.² Mersault, the main character in Camus's *The Stranger*, draws the community's ire for failing to cry at his mother's funeral, and this later serves as evidence against him at trial. Mersault has many faults (chiefly, murder), but dry eyes are not one of them. Indeed, many of us would describe such a person as "grieving in their own way."

But notice that this generous remark contains a crucial assumption: that grief—however it manifests itself—is the appropriate response to the death of one's mother. Even if emotions are not within our *full* control, there are at least two important senses in which they are more or less reasonable. First, it matters *which* emotion gets felt. The loss of one's child or spouse makes Louise and Fuwaad's grief appropriate—it would be inappropriate if either were overjoyed. Second, the *strength* of the emotion matters. Though spilling milk may be mildly upsetting, it's nothing to cry over.³ Both aspects determine whether our emotions are reasonable.

The reasonableness of our emotions also yields rich philosophical upshots. Many of our emotions—resentment, love, joy, and grief—reveal important things about the world. For instance, P.F. Strawson (1962) thought that resentment provides evidence of freedom. Our resentment toward someone who does wrong—like Fuwaad's self-resentment over his harsh words to his wife—can only be appropriate if the person deserves blame, which in turn requires that they freely did wrong. More recently, Myisha Cherry (2020) defends rage as an important emotion that responds to injustice. But rage, resentment, and the like can only play these roles if they reasonably respond to the world. If these emotions weren't responding to anything, they would not tell us anything about the world.

16.2 Are Events Permanent?

A second response to the puzzle denies (2), which claims that events are permanent parts of the world. The core idea is that events fade into the past. Sometimes, people mean this in a very literal sense. Only the present, they'll say, is real. It's all we have, for the past (and the future) literally don't exist. But if past events don't exist, how can we explain the reasonability of emotions directed toward them? Instead, we would expect our

---

²There's an interesting analogy to belief. Like our emotions, belief often lies out of our control, yet beliefs are still reasonable (such as when they match our available evidence) and unreasonable (such as when they don't match our evidence).

³Justin D'Arms and David Jacobson (2000) call these two aspects the "size" and "shape" of emotions. They also provide further argument for emotions as (un)reasonable responses to events in the world.

emotions to evaporate, because there wouldn't be anything in the world for them to respond to.

But this obviously can't be right. First, the metaphysical worldview could be wrong. In "The Merchant and the Alchemist's Gate," the past and future are as real as the present. Characters like Fuwaad can travel to them through gates just as easily as they can travel to neighboring towns. Indeed, according to *eternalism* (the view of time that physicists like Einstein endorse), time is a dimension like space. Saying that only the present exists is like saying that only a particular place exists. Second, even if the past and future do not exist, that doesn't explain the *gradual* recession of emotions.[4] Grief is a process, and it doesn't vanish as soon as an event vanishes into the past. Third, regardless of whether they exist, past and future events affect our present states. The death of Fuwaad's wife follows him for 20 years. The future moves Louise to both joy and grief. Similarly, anyone who has witnessed a loved one die gradually knows that grief can start before the actual death and continues long after it. This grief is appropriate, regardless of whether the event, strictly speaking, exists.

Perhaps a better version of this response focuses on our distance from the events in question rather than their existence. The further removed we are from a death, the more fitting it is for grief to subside. This explains why we think some people need to "let go." For instance, while Captain Ahab's anger might have been appropriate immediately after his first encounter with Moby Dick, the endurance and intensity of his anger are unreasonable and constitute his central character flaw. Our temporal distance from an event often explains the appropriateness of the strength of our emotions. The best case for this is Fuwaad's return to the past. Fuwaad inadvertently intercepts the messenger who would have comforted his past self with news about his wife's last words—that "while her life was short, it was made happy by the time she spent with [him]" (Chiang 2019, 34). It would have been too easy for young Fuwaad to receive this news. In fact, we might judge that it would have been inappropriate for young Fuwaad to release his self-resentment so soon after his harsh last words to his wife. Only after 20 years is it appropriate for older Fuwaad's self-resentment to recede after hearing his wife's words.

This version of the second response is better, but it's still incorrect. The timing of Fuwaad's discovery about his wife doesn't fully explain the

---

[4] Thanks to Mark Balaguer for this point.

reasonableness of the change in his emotions. *What* he's done during that time is also relevant:

> I [Fuwaad] repented and atoned as best I knew how; for twenty years I lived as an upright man, I offered prayers and fasted and gave alms to those less fortunate and made a pilgrimage to Mecca, and yet I was still haunted by guilt. (ibid., 29)

His regret and resentment, plus the steps he's taken while seeking atonement, matter. To appreciate this point, imagine an alternate world in which Fuwaad feels some regret and resentment, but continues engaging in the slave trade without attempting to atone. If this alt-Fuwaad goes back in time and learns of his wife's words, redemption isn't appropriate. While time might enable one to sufficiently atone so that receding resentment is appropriate, time alone is insufficient.

The same holds for Louise, whose encounter with Heptapod B changes her temporal experiences:

> I experience past and future all at once; my consciousness becomes a half-century-long ember burning outside time. I perceive—during those glimpses—that the entire epoch as a simultaneity. It's a period encompassing the rest of my life, and the entirety of yours. (Chiang 2002, 141)

Her emotions presumably don't change over time since her experience encompasses all of time. Even though her daughter's birth and death lie in the future, her joy and grief are just as strong now as they will be when those events occur because she perceives that "entire epoch as a simultaneity." The stories about Fuwaad and Louise suggest that our temporal distance from events can't fully explain why it often appears appropriate for our emotions to change over time.

16.3 Are Changes in Emotions Rational?

The final way of dissolving the puzzle rejects (3), the claim that a change in emotions often is reasonable. Instead, the most reasonable emotional response requires us to retain our emotions permanently. Since our emotions match events in the world, and those events don't change, our emotions should not change. Louise's experience of time supports this response. Her emotional reactions to events remain unchanged because she continually sees the events before her. Grief is always fitting because the death of her child is etched into the world.

In a way, Louise's emotional life parallels the advice Buddhist monks sometimes offer to those who are grieving. (I received such advice at my grandmother's funeral, and I confess it may subconsciously influence my interest in this puzzle.) Because everything is impermanent, death and loss are inevitable. Interestingly, the Buddhist advice that arises from acknowledging this inevitability is that we ought never grieve. The appropriate response to impermanence is unattachment, even in the immediate aftermath of a loved one's death. Obviously, people differ on whether unattachment or grief is the appropriate response to death. The Stoics said something similar to Buddhists (though for different reasons), and I suspect that modern Western sentiments sympathize with Louise's grief. But crucially, these very different takes on the appropriateness of grief agree that whatever the appropriate emotional response is, it should be felt across all times and remain unchanged.

However, this response faces one major challenge: it flies in the face of how people *actually* experience emotions and what we commonly judge to be appropriate. Many people don't grieve indefinitely; they often move on surprisingly quickly. Indeed, people who don't stop grieving are clinically diagnosed with depression. The same holds for other emotions. Ahab's enduring anger is pathological—precisely because it never diminishes. We don't often observe enduring emotions, and when we do, they often seem inappropriate or at least striking. Thus, this response faces the challenge of explaining why "moving on" is so common and widely accepted.

16.4 Tentative Conclusions

I'd like to close by offering a tentative suggestion: that Ted Chiang's stories favor rejecting (3) rather than (1) or (2). That is, his stories suggest that it's often inappropriate for our emotions to change even though people widely believe that such changes are appropriate! I also will offer an explanation for why it *appears* appropriate for emotions to change, even though that's not actually the case.

First, the stories provide reasons to embrace (1) and (2). The reasonableness of emotions, (1), drives Fuwaad and Louise. Fuwaad's self-resentment and regret over his last words to his wife shapes the rest of his life. Louise's eternal love and grief for her daughter makes the story of her life all the more powerful since she chooses the future with her daughter with full knowledge of the highest highs and lowest lows.

Furthermore, how Fuwaad and Louise experience time reinforces (2), the idea that events are eternal. Fuwaad and the others who pass through the alchemist's gates have their reasons for love and regret reinforced as they more fully discover their pasts and futures. Louise knows exactly how and when her daughter dies, and that permanent and inevitable event—along with all the other ones composing her daughter's life—makes her grief reasonable, regardless of how far into the past or future it is.

Finally, the stories favor rejecting (3) and embracing the reasonableness of enduring emotions instead. But what about our own emotional lives? We don't experience time as Chiang's characters do. Can refusing to change our emotions be the right solution for us? I humbly propose that it is. As with Louise and Fuwaad, our enduring emotions are reasonable. However, our emotions don't always endure in quite the same way, so we need to *explain why* this is.

Consider first how our experiences differ from Louise's. While she simultaneously experiences the past, present, and future, we typically only experience the present. As beings imprisoned in linear time, events unfold for us one by one. Even so, we sometimes remember or anticipate events and then feel corresponding emotions. Anniversaries of both death and celebratory occasions provoke grief and joy, as does visiting a significant place or catching a familiar scent. In these cases, we re-experience events and emotions that match as well as they did before. Put another way, it's never inappropriate to feel love and sorrow when remembering the dearly departed. Our emotion *can* appropriately endure. But our psychology—which unlike Louise does not keep all events in our mind's eye—prevents us from doing so.

Next, consider how multiple events, each corresponding to different emotions, interact with each other for Louise and Fuwaad. Louise is aware of past, present, and future events simultaneously and feels all corresponding emotions at once. When Fuwaad revisits the past, the discovery of his wife's forgiveness, combined with his longstanding attempt to atone, shows him that releasing his resentment and regret is appropriate. The beauty of his story is that the events justifying both resentment and forgiveness are always there—he just isn't always aware of them. Our experiences are closer to Fuwaad's than Louise's. Our lives contain a multitude of events and emotions. When we think of someone like Ahab, who feels only rage and vengeance for the rest of his life, we know that something is missing. It's appropriate to be angry that a whale took his leg and killed his crew, but it's inappropriate to fail to appreciate all other aspects of his life. When an emotion fits an event, it *always* fits. But because there are so many events in our lives, to be consumed by just one, and feel just one corresponding emotion, is unreasonable.[5] Thus, our emotions change because (a) our lives contain many events and thus a range of appropriate emotional responses, and (b) we are the type of beings who psychologically entertain a limited number of events.

To be sure, some may find this conclusion unsettling. The reasonableness of eternal grief sounds quite daunting! But alongside that grief, we find that all of our reasons for love, joy, and what makes life worth living endure eternally as well. That is all, and perhaps that is more than enough.

Acknowledgments I'd like to thank David Friedell for organizing the most wonderful conference on Ted Chiang and philosophy and putting this anthology together. He and the other workshop participants—including Ted Chiang!—provided invaluable feedback on early ideas for this chapter. I'd also like to thank Amy Seymour and Brian Ballard for their workshops in which this chapter more fully took shape. Mark Balaguer, Kenneth Davis, and David Friedell gave careful comments on early drafts, for which I'm deeply appreciative. Finally, I dedicate this chapter to Ponyo, who showed me that love, like grief, never ends.

References

Cherry, Myisha. 2020. *The Case for Rage*. Oxford: Oxford University Press.
Chiang, Ted. 2002. Story of Your Life. In *Story of Your Life and Others*, 91–146. New York: Vintage Books.
———. 2019. The Merchant and the Alchemist's Gate. In *Exhalation*, 3–36. New York: Vintage Books.
D'Arms, Justin, and David Jacobson. 2000. The Moralistic Fallacy: On the 'Appropriateness of Emotions'. *Philosophy and Phenomenological Research* 61 (1): 65–90.
Marušić, Berislav. 2022. *On the Temporality of Emotions*. Oxford: Oxford University Press.
Strawson, P. F. 1962. Freedom and Resentment. *Proceedings of the British Academy* 48:1–25.

---

[5] Again, consider the analogy between emotions and belief. Imagine a person who only focused on believing that 2+2=4. That belief is appropriate because it's true, and it's eternally appropriate and true. But focusing on only that one belief and ignoring the infinitely many other truths would be inappropriate, just as feeling only one emotion in response to one event would be. Thanks to Brian Ballard for this point.

PART IX

Human and Alien Intelligence

CHAPTER 17

Language, Thought, Experience, and Chiang's "Story of Your Life"

Peter Murray

17.1 Introduction

In philosophy, it is often said, everything connects with everything. By that measure, Ted Chiang's award-winning novella "Story of Your Life" is a quintessential piece of philosophy. It ingeniously connects issues in the philosophy of language and mind to issues in the metaphysics of time, which it in turn connects to whether free will is compatible with knowledge of one's future and ultimately to existential questions of how best to live in the face of inevitability. However, the whole novella arguably turns around a perennially fascinating idea about the relationship between language, thought, and our experience of the world.

Earth has been visited by alien "Heptapods," and the task of the main character, linguist Louise Banks, is to decipher the aliens' distinct spoken and written languages ("Heptapod A" and "Heptapod B," respectively). Louise's breakthrough comes when she realizes that, unlike human languages, Heptapod B is "nonlinear": meaningful expressions in Heptapod B—from individual words to whole disquisitions—come all at once in a

---

P. Murray (✉)
Department of Philosophy, Skidmore College, Saratoga Springs, NY, USA
e-mail: pmurray@skidmore.edu

© The Author(s), under exclusive license to Springer Nature
Switzerland AG 2025
D. Friedell (ed.), *The Philosophy of Ted Chiang*,
https://doi.org/10.1007/978-3-031-81662-8_17

single complex figure or "semagram." The meaning of everything in a semagram connects to, and depends on, everything else in the semagram, with no sequence or priority among its constituents.

Furthermore, Louise discovers, Heptapod B reflects the Heptapods' non-sequential, non-causal experience of the world. For them, there is no before and after, no cause and effect. Rather, for Heptapods, all of time and space, and every event that has or ever will take place, form a single, eternal "block universe" of which we may experience only a part, but all of which already exists to be experienced. Finally, and most dramatically, Louise's burgeoning fluency in Heptapod B enables her to experience the world as the Heptapods do. Indeed, this ability to experience her past, present, and future enables Louise to write the titular "Story of Your Life" both to and about her as-yet unborn daughter.

This idea of "linguistic relativity"—the idea that the particular language one uses can shape how one thinks and experiences the world—has been the focus of centuries of philosophical debate. French Enlightenment thinkers like Condillac and Rousseau defended versions of linguistic relativity, as did the German Counter-Enlightenment figures Herder and Hamann, the Romantics Schlegel and von Humboldt, and the American anthropologists and linguists Boas, Sapir, and Whorf in the early twentieth century, among others. In the latter half of the twentieth century, linguistic relativity fell into disfavor under the influence of Chomsky's work in linguistics. However, a new generation of anthropologists, linguists, psychologists, and philosophers have been using empirical techniques to raise the debate from the level of mere speculation into the realm of testable hypotheses with important philosophical implications.

In this chapter, we will consider the contemporary debate around linguistic relativity, and we will assess the current state of that debate, both empirically and philosophically.

17.2 Linguistic Relativity: From Intuitions to Empirically Testable Claim

The capacities for new forms of thought and experience that Louise acquires through learning Heptapod B make for particularly dramatic fiction. However, it does seem improbable that merely learning a new language—even an alien language—could enable someone to experience their future and so remember it now. Moreover, the very idea of such a capacity presupposes certain things that may not be true, including that my future already exists for me to experience, such that I could, at least in principle, remember it now.

We are not going to settle the nature of time here, nor the question of whether I can remember my own future. More importantly, we do not need to appeal to such speculative cases to motivate the idea of linguistic relativity. For example, second-language learners commonly describe thinking differently in their new language, as compared to their native language. Novel inferences and associations can strike us as natural when using a second language, even if they would not occur to us at all in our first language. We find we must attend to different aspects of the world, if we are to inhabit our new language's sometimes radically different system of person, case, gender, tense, aspect, mood, number, evidentiality (justification for a statement), mirativity (degree of surprise), and/or other features that may exist in one language but not in the other. And this felt sense of thinking differently, depending on which language one is speaking, tends only to intensify after we cross that Rubicon of fluency where, as we say, we stop thinking in our first language, and instead are able to think and express ourselves in our new language directly. Indeed, many multilingual people report feeling they have a whole different personality or self, depending on the language they are speaking.[1]

Such self-reports and felt experiences do not by themselves show that linguistic relativity is true. After all, people can misunderstand why they have certain experiences, misidentify—even invert—cause and effect, and/or mistake a mere correlation for a causal relationship. So, what could show that linguistic relativity is true?

The contemporary consensus is that strong evidence for three interrelated claims is required to show that linguistic relativity is true:

1. *Linguistic diversity*: there are differences between languages, such as differences in vocabularies and/or grammars, that could conceivably cause differences in how their speakers think or experience the world;
2. *Correlated cognitive diversity*: given evidence that two languages are diverse, there are correlated differences in how their speakers think and/or experience the world, differences that are "non-linguistic,"

---

[1] Pavlenko, Aneta. 2011. *Thinking and Speaking in Two Languages*. Bristol: Multilingual Matters.

i.e., that do not consist simply in the differences between their respective languages;
3. *Causality*: given evidence of a correlation between linguistic diversity and cognitive diversity, the former causes—and is not merely correlated with—the latter.

Before turning to some of the evidence for these claims, it is worth making three clarifications. First, Claim (1) is already widely accepted because the evidence for such linguistic diversity is overwhelming.[2] For example, the languages of the Pirahã and Mundurukú peoples do not have a system of numbers beyond "3," and speakers of such languages find it difficult to perform tasks which require that they keep track of and distinguish between, say, a group of six items and a group of seven items.[3]

Second, the stipulation in Claim (2) that the evidence for cognitive diversity be non-linguistic is important to avoid the following argumentative circularity: "What is the evidence that speakers of two languages think and experience the world differently? Well, just look at the differences in their languages!" Contemporary research on linguistic relativity therefore generally tests participants' performance on tasks that do not involve speaking. However, it is also well recognized that someone who is not speaking aloud to perform a task may nevertheless be subvocalizing—i.e., "speaking" silently to themselves—so as to perform the task, and here the threat of argumentative circularity looms again. Accordingly, many researchers include "verbal interference" conditions in their experiments, such as having participants repeat nonsense syllables while performing a non-verbal task. This interference minimizes the chance that speakers even unconsciously employ language as an aid in performing the task.

Finally, linguistic relativity must be sharply distinguished from another position that has now generally been abandoned. According to the abandoned position—call it "Linguistic Determinism"—if language A does not have equivalents to words or grammatical constructions that language B uses to express certain thoughts, then thinking the latter thoughts is simply *impossible* for speakers of language A. According to Linguistic Determinism, speakers of diverse languages are thus trapped inside

---

[2] Evans, Nicholas, and Stephen Levinson. 2009. The Myth of Language Universals. *Behavioral and Brain Sciences* 32, no. 5: 429–48.

[3] Pitt, Benjamin, Edward Gibson, and Steven T. Piantadosi. 2022. Exact Number Concepts Are Limited to the Verbal Count Range. *Psychological Science* 33, no. 3: 371–81.

cognitive "bubbles" of their respective languages' making. They are forever cut off from genuine communication with each other and, indeed, from experiencing or knowing the world as speakers of another language do, inasmuch as our respective languages give us the concepts with which we experience, understand, think, and talk about the world.

However, none of this is part of the linguistic relativity hypothesis. What linguistic relativity hypothesizes is that the diverse features of different languages encourage, reinforce, and otherwise cause us to default into certain habits of thought and experience: what we tend to think about, ignore, pay attention to, remember, and/or how we categorize what we encounter in the world. There is no inkling here of the idea that speakers of one language cannot think or express thoughts that speakers of another language can.

17.3 Contemporary Empirical Research on Linguistic Relativity

Contemporary empirical research on linguistic relativity encompasses a wide and constantly expanding range of topics, only a sliver of which can be mentioned here.[4] In addition to the case mentioned above of languages without exact large numbers, another seminal area of research addresses how differing sets of color words across languages affects people's experience of hues.[5] Other work shows that people tend to group objects together differently according to whether they speak: (1) a language, such as English or French, that distinguishes between "count" nouns like *dog* and *shoe*, which refer to particular items, and "mass" nouns like *water* and *dirt* that refer to a kind of stuff; or (2) a language, such as Japanese or Mandarin, that treats all nouns like mass nouns, requiring the use of a "classifier" like *piece of* in order to count anything. Experiments show that speakers of count-mass languages tend to group objects according to shape, whereas speakers of classifier languages tend to group objects according to material.[6]

---

[4] Everett, Caleb. 2013. *Linguistic Relativity*. Boston: De Gruyter Mouton.

[5] Lupyan, Gary, Rasha Abdel Rahman, Lera Boroditsky, and Andy Clark. 2020. Effects of Language on Visual Perception. *Trends in Cognitive Sciences* 24, no. 11: 930–44.

[6] Imai, Mutsumi, and Reiko Mazuka. 2003. Reevaluating Linguistic Relativity. In *Language in Mind*, edited by Dedre Gentner and Susan Goldin-Meadow, 429–64. Cambridge, MA: MIT Press.

Another important research program focuses on differences in how various languages treat space. For example, languages such as Guugu Yimithirr and Tzeltal utilize "absolute" coordinates—north, south, east, west—instead of the "egocentric" frame of reference—left, right, front, back—preferred in languages like English, Dutch, and Japanese. In absolute-orientation languages, one would not be asked to move one's *left* hand *forward* but instead to move one's *eastern* hand *north*, and one would likewise be told that butter can be found along the *west*—rather than the *right*—wall of the store. Moreover, these linguistic differences show up in non-linguistic behavior. For example, in experiments where participants are presented with a set of objects in a certain linear order, and then the participants are rotated 180 degrees, given the same objects, and asked to place them in the same order as before, the differences are striking: speakers of absolute-orientation languages tend to place objects in the same east-west-north-south order they previously observed, while speakers of egocentric-orientation languages place objects in the same left-to-right order, relative to themselves, 180 degrees out of phase to how the speakers of absolute-orientation languages place them.[7]

A final line of empirical research to mention here connects with the question in "Story of Your Life" of how language shapes our conceptualization of time. In the vast majority of languages, time is spatialized and treated as a line with a particular orientation. In English, it is common to talk about the future as "in front" or "ahead" of us, the past as what we've "gone through" or what's "behind us," and of events as having a "long" or "short" duration. This pattern can also be found in languages as different as Russian and Dutch, among others.

However, even in languages that spatialize time as a line, the orientation of that line varies dramatically. In Aymara and Vietnamese, for example, the past, which we know, is what we can see before us, and the future, which is unknown, is behind us.[8] In Mandarin, by contrast, the line is vertical, with earlier events above us, and later events below.[9] And in absolute-orientation languages like Kuuk Thaayorre, time stretches from

---

[7] Majid, Asifa, Melissa Bowerman, Sotaro Kita, Daniel B. M. Haun, and Stephen C. Levinson. 2004. Can Language Restructure Cognition? The Case for Space. *Trends in Cognitive Sciences* 8, no. 3: 108–14.

[8] Sullivan, Karen, and Linh Thuy Bui. 2016. With the Future Coming Up Behind Them. *Cognitive Linguistics* 27, no. 2: 205–33.

[9] Boroditsky, Lera, Orly Fuhrman, and Kelly McCormick. 2011. Do English and Mandarin Speakers Think about Time Differently? *Cognition* 118, no. 1: 123–29.

the past in the east into the future in the west.[10] These linguistic differences manifest in their speakers' behavior in ways consistent with linguistic relativity, as shown in experiments requiring participants to arrange a series of cards depicting earlier and later stages of an event. Speakers of Kuuk Thaayorre consistently arrange the cards so the earliest stages of the event are east-most, and later stages are placed successively westward, regardless of whether participants are facing east, west, north, or south. By contrast, English speakers arrange the cards from left to right, a habit that appears related to the English practice of writing from left to right, whereas speakers of Hebrew, which is written from right to left, tend correspondingly to arrange the cards from right to left.[11]

Moreover, there are languages, such as Greek or Spanish, that tend not to spatialize time as a line but instead treat it as a quantity of which there is much or little. This difference, too, has been used to show that language shapes how speakers conceptualize time. In one experiment, English speakers and Greek speakers watched two different sets of animations. In one set, lines grew longer over a certain period of time, but the period of time and the length of the lines were systematically varied: in some animations, a long line grew to its full length over a short period of time; in others, a short line grew to its full length over a long period of time; and so on. In the other series of animations, buckets filled with water over a certain period of time, and, as before, the amount of water in the bucket and the period of time during which the bucket filled were systematically varied. Participants were instructed to use mouse clicks to indicate either the duration of the animation or the length of the line/fill level of the bucket. As predicted by linguistic relativity, English and Greek speakers performed differently on the task. English speakers tended to be affected by the length of the line: they overestimated the time it took for longer lines to grow to full length, and they underestimated the time it took shorter lines to grow to full length, but they were unaffected by the fill level in the bucket animations. Greek speakers showed the opposite effect: the fill level of the bucket distorted their judgments of duration, but the length of the line did not.[12]

---

[10] Boroditsky, Lera, and Alice Gaby. 2010. Remembrances of Times East. *Psychological Science* 21, no. 11: 1635–1639.

[11] Fuhrman, Orly, and Lera Boroditsky. 2010. Cross-Cultural Differences in Mental Representations of Time. *Cognitive Science* 34, no. 8: 1430–51.

[12] Casasanto, Daniel, and Lera Boroditsky. 2008. Time in the Mind. *Cognition* 106, no. 2: 579–93.

17.4 Conclusion: Empirical and Philosophical Assessment of Linguistic Relativity

So, what are we to make of these experimental results in relation to the linguistic relativity hypothesis? The work is obviously still ongoing, even accelerating, some particular results have failed to replicate, and some interpretations of the data have been challenged. However, in aggregate, the empirical case for Claim (2) of linguistic relativity—that linguistic differences correlate with cognitive differences among speakers—seems undeniable. Moreover, the evidence for Claim (3)—that linguistic diversity causes cognitive diversity—continues to mount as researchers refine their experimental techniques.[13] One recent source of evidence for Claim (3) is neuroscientific experiments that demonstrate the effects that speaking different languages has on the operation of the brain, even in non-linguistic contexts.[14]

Philosophically, there is dispute over the significance of linguistic relativity research. Some insist that only evidence for the truth of something like Linguistic Determinism would be philosophically noteworthy, and so they dismiss the experimental results as "banal" and "uninteresting."[15] However, this reaction is tendentious and unwarranted. It is of unalloyed philosophical and scientific importance to study and document the strikingly different ways in which people think about and experience the world, as well as the connections between linguistic and cognitive diversity. Such work grounds a more accurate understanding of the full landscape of our multiform human nature and helps correct the homogenizing distortions in that understanding introduced by the long-standing economic, scientific, social, and linguistic hegemony of so-called WEIRD—Western, Educated, Industrialized, Rich, and Democratic—societies.[16] Moreover, the relevant work is urgent: under pressure from globalization and other forces, 42 percent of the world's approximately 7000 languages—and typically the smallest and most diverse among them—are endangered and

---

[13] Casasanto, Daniel. 2016. Linguistic Relativity. In *The Routledge Handbook of Semantics*, edited by Nick Riemer, 158–74. New York: Routledge.

[14] Athanasopoulos, Panos, and Aina Casaponsa. 2020. The Whorfian Brain: Neuroscientific Approaches to Linguistic Relativity. *Cognitive Neuropsychology* 37, no. 5–6: 393–412.

[15] Pinker, Steven. 2007. *The Stuff of Thought*. New York: Viking Press.

[16] Henrich, Joseph, Steven J. Heine, and Ara Norenzayan. 2010. The Weirdest People in the World? *Behavioral and Brain Sciences* 33, no. 2–3: 61–83.

going extinct at the rate of approximately one every 40 days, many without having been fully documented.[17]

There is, of course, no foregone conclusion about what linguistic relativity research will reveal about human beings, and we need philosophers, psychologists, anthropologists, sociologists, linguists, economists, neurologists, and others to collaboratively refine our understanding of the areas in which we are different from each other, and the ways in which we are alike. In this domain, as in so many others—and as in Chiang's "Story of Your Life"—everything connects with everything.[18]

---

[17] Simons, Gary F. 2019. Two Centuries of Spreading Language Loss. *Proceedings of the Linguistic Society of America* 4: 27:1–12.

[18] I thank Marta Brunner, David Friedell, Ruth McAdams, Alexis Shotwell, Eileen Sperry, and Erica Wojcik for their invaluable help in preparing this chapter.

CHAPTER 18

Jeopardy! and the Stories of Our Lives

Benjamin Chan

18.1 INSOMNIA

On a frigid Wisconsin night in January 2024, I am startled awake by a sudden and very specific worry. It's not about my aging furnace, though it should be. Instead, I'm gripped by the realization that I can't recall the name of the river that runs through Warsaw. My mind suggests it starts with a "V" … and keeps filling in "Vltava," but that's Prague's river. Nor is it Vilnius—that's the capital of Lithuania. I struggle, attempting to unearth the name that should fit snugly into the gap in my consciousness where Warsaw's river belongs. After a few minutes, I concede defeat and reach for the world atlas on my nightstand, finally uncovering the elusive name: the Vistula.

Why was there an atlas on my nightstand? More importantly, why was my inability to retrieve the name of a river in a city that I have no intention of visiting a source of insomniac anxiety? The culprit? Jeopardy! The long-running television quiz show where contestants are presented with clues in the form of an answer and must answer in the form of a question had seeped into my subconscious. In spring of 2023, I was chosen to appear

---

B. Chan (✉)
Green Bay, WI, USA
e-mail: benjaminmhchan@gmail.com

on the show and had an eventful nine-game winning streak, making me the 16th-winningest contestant in the game's history.[1] Those victories earned me a spot in the prestigious Tournament of Champions in 2024, which was the root of my sleepless night. Along this journey, my perspective on the show shifted from viewing it as a simple test of knowledge to recognizing its celebration of life's contingency. My embrace of contingency has shaped my reading of Ted Chiang's "Understand," with echoes of the synoptic vision of existence presented in Chiang's "The Story of Your Life."

18.2 THE WORD

"Understand" follows the cognitive enhancement of Greco and his estrangement from non-enhanced people as he attains superintelligence. Greco is ultimately brought down by Reynolds, who has also been made super-intelligent by his use of "hormone K." Greco is an aesthete who is gripped by the "blinding, joyous, fearful symmetry" he now sees in the universe and is on a quest to comprehend the "ultimate gestalt … the context in which all knowledge fits and is illuminated" (55). Reynolds, a philanthropist and pragmatist, simply wants "to save the world, to protect it from itself" (62). The two are drawn into conflict because Greco's plan to attain transcendent awareness requires marshaling computing resources that are at odds with Reynolds's design for world peace. Their showdown does not involve guns, knives, or fisticuffs. Instead, each attempts to disable the other by hacking the other's brain.

Reynolds emerges as the victor, having planted a self-destruct mechanism that is triggered by "the Word":

> The Word: the sentence that, when uttered, would destroy the mind of the listener. Reynolds Is claiming that the myth is true, that every mind has such a trigger built in; that for every person, there is a sentence that can reduce him to an idiot, a lunatic, a catatonic. (67)

This idea of a cognitive self-destruct command occurs elsewhere in science fiction. In Christopher Cherniak's "The Riddle of the Universe and

---

[1] I was the first contestant to win their first nine games in "runaways," meaning that I could skip the final round and still be guaranteed a victory. In my tenth game, I lost controversially, when I wrote that "Beatrice and Benedict" were the couple from *Much Ado About Nothing* and was ruled incorrect ("Benedick" is the preferred spelling).

its Solution," any person who encounters the Riddle lapses into an irreversible coma, so the contents of the Riddle can of course not be shared with the story's readers! Douglas Hofstadter observes that the coma-inducing Riddle is reminiscent of the Monty Python sketch "about a joke so funny that anyone who hears it will literally die laughing" or Arthur C. Clarke's story about a tune so catchy it takes over the mind of anyone who hears it or the siren song of myth that lured sailors to their doom (Hofstadter 276).

Unlike Cherniak's Riddle, Chiang doesn't simply leave the Word entirely up to our imagination—he tells us what it is: "understand." When Greco is told this magic, destructive word—understand—he is surprised that it is a memory trigger, eliciting a series of perceptions that Reynolds had staged in Greco's environment in the preceding days—an image on the t-shirt of a man at a grocery store here, a sound in his apartment there. These sights and sounds recalled from memory combine just so to unravel Greco: "I comprehend the Word, and the means by which it operates, and so I dissolve" (70). Unlike Cherniak's Riddle or Clarke's earworm it does not work on just any listener. It is not a devious logical paradox that paralyzes any thinker who is adept and unlucky enough to parse it. "Understand" undoes Greco by putting him in touch with a contingent series of perceptions particular to his experience of the world in the preceding days. In short, Greco's quest for transcendence is uprooted when he is made aware of specific contingencies of his existence. His demise is enabled by the fact that, with his preoccupation on the sublime, he has neglected the reality that being embodied means being situated in a particular time and place.

18.3 Contingency

Coincidentally, Logan Pearsall Smith, who happened to be the brother-in-law of Bertrand Russell, also writes of the mind-stopping impact of "the Word" on his understanding of a comprehensive understanding of the Universe:

> When I looked up at the Stars, the great Stars that bore me company, streaming over the dark houses as I moved; I felt that I was the Lord of Life the mystery and disquieting meaninglessness of existence the existence of other people, and of my own, were solved for me now [...]
> And then the Word struck me; the Word people would use. I stopped in the street; my Soul was silenced like a bell that snarls at a jarring touch [...]

> Away with that police-force of brutal words which bursts in on our best moments and arrests our finest feelings! (Smith 119–20)

The only reason I know about this passage is because it appears in Smith's collection of short reflections entitled Trivia, originally published in 1902. According to the OED, Smith is thereby responsible for the earliest known use of "trivia" as an English noun. "Trivia," in turn, derives from the Latin trivium, which has a few different meanings. It can refer to three foundational subjects of the liberal arts: grammar, logic, and rhetoric. It can also mean "crossroads"—literally, a place where three roads meet (tri and via). Some contestants dislike referring to Jeopardy! as trivia, fearing that it connotes unimportance. However, I adore the word, because I think a crossroad is an apt metaphor for the show. Crossroads are places of contingency, and there are at least three facets of contingency that the quiz show has illuminated for me: the accidents, biography, and convergence.

Jeopardy! celebrates the accidental through its peculiar answer-then-question format. Take the question, "What is 300?" For Greco, who is surrounded by "blinding, joyous, fearful symmetry," we would expect answers that get to the essence of 300. Perhaps:

- It is the number whose factorization is 2 * 2 * 3 * 5 * 5.
- It is a triangular number.
- It is the sum of a pair of the twin primes 149 + 151.

By contrast, here are some of the ways the writers of Jeopardy! have "answered" the question, "What is 300?"[2]

- It is a perfect score in bowling, or the length of a football field in feet.
- It is the number of degrees that the minute hand of your watch passes through between 2:00 pm and 2:50 pm.
- It is the title of a movie for which Michael Fassbender dieted on cottage cheese.

---

[2] These answers appeared on episodes that aired on October 12, 2023, April 27, 2020, and October 20, 2016 and were retrieved from the invaluable J! Archive site (https://j-archive.com), a "fan-created archive of Jeopardy! games and players."

The web of knowledge constituted by the show's answer-then-question format is knit together by messy coincidence, accident, and happenstance, not rapturous symmetries.

The second contingency that Jeopardy! highlights is in its contestants: knowledge acquisition is biographical. Psychologist Monica Thieu—winner of the 2012 College Championship—noticed that fellow contestants could often remember exactly where they learned a fact. All-time great contestant Ken Jennings observed that he could often remember with great specificity where he learned a fact, "in which book or magazine from my elementary school library—even down to what part of the page" (Thieu et al. 2024: 1). Thieu, along with colleagues Lauren Wilkins and Mariam Aly, conducted an experiment on the acquisition of new facts. Their findings suggested stronger links between the biographical memory of specific events and the acquisition of general knowledge in trivia experts compared to non-experts (Thieu et al. 1).

For instance, I encountered this $1000 clue in the category RESTAURANTS (May 18, 2023):

> CARMY ON "THE BEAR" PREVIOUSLY WORKED AT THIS MUCH-AWARDED THOMAS KELLER RESTAURANT THAT'S IN CALIFORNIA, NOT EUROPE

Although I have watched "The Bear," I don't remember Carmy's employment history. However, 24 years ago, in the Hallowell dormitory at Swarthmore College, my friend Walter showed me instructions for blanching vegetables. Instructions for blanching vegetables should not be memorable, but these were. According to this new cookbook, blanching vegetables requires what seemed to me a truly alarming amount of water. Quarts and quarts for just a handful of green beans, lest the water temperature drop when the vegetables are immersed, and the color of the beans muddied. This extravagant cookbook featured a crisp white napkin on its cover, cementing the restaurant's name in my memory. Twenty-four years later, I say: "What is the French Laundry?" and am somehow $1000 richer for remembering this.[3]

---

[3] How far would the $1000 go at the French Laundry? At the time of writing, its least expensive prix fixe meal is $390 per person, the most expensive is $1200, not including "add-ons."

Finally, Jeopardy! effectively highlights notable convergences in history through its clues as it provides contestants with multiple pathways to the correct response. Contestants need all the help we can get! Typically, 60 answers and questions are completed within a mere 13 minutes of real-time gameplay. This translates to approximately 12 seconds for the host to read the clue, a contestant to respond, and then select the next clue. I found myself needing to decide within two or three seconds of the clue's unveiling whether to buzz in, and I needed to be at 90% confidence to feel comfortable with my attempt. That is not a lot of time. Players can respond quickly and competently due in large part to the fact that there is usually more than one clue embedded in a single clue.

For instance, take this clue in the category RUSSIAN AROUND (April 12, 2008):

> LEO TOLSTOY GOT A FIRSTHAND LOOK AT WAR AT SEVASTAPOL DURING THIS WAR

Within two or three seconds, I might not be 90% confident that Sevastapol is in Crimea, or 90% confident that I had heard that Tolstoy had fought in Crimea, or 90% confident that Tolstoy's date of birth puts him at prime military age at the time of that war. However, as my brain simultaneously takes these three helpful pathways provided by the writers, I can very quickly be 90% sure that one of those three things is true and conclude that "What Is the Crimean War?" the correct response. At the same time, the writers have shown us how three canonical elements of geography, military history, and literary biography converge: in Sevastopol, during the Crimean War, in the person of Tolstoy.

18.4 Pragmatism

When Greco realizes that Reynolds has gotten the best of him, he admires his rival's "ingenuity," remarking that "pragmatism avails a savior far more than aestheticism" (70). At the same time, he struggles to grasp why Reynolds would choose to align himself with ordinary humanity and relinquish the pursuit of transcendent beauty. I think Reynolds's pragmatism goes beyond mere ingenuity. In identifying with the fate of non-enhanced human beings, and rejecting the aspiration for transcendence, Reynolds seems to me firmly the philosophical tradition of American Pragmatism. There is no justification from the point of view of eternity necessary for caring about the world and the people in it. As Reynolds puts it, "as long as you and I can still comprehend their affairs, we can't ignore them" (65). This world-loving sentiment is echoed by the pragmatist Richard Rorty, relating Walt Whitman's hopes that his countrymen embrace curiosity:

> Americans, he hoped, would spend the energy that past human societies had spent on discovering God's desires on discovering one another's desires. Americans will be curious about every other American, but not about anything which claims authority over America. (Rorty 1998: 16)

Notably, the winner of the 2024 Tournament of Champions, Yogesh Raut, claims his success is inextricable from a deep curiosity borne of necessity:

> I had to prove every day that I was an American [...] I quickly became attuned to listening to others, finding out what they cared about, and developing ways of having conversations about those things despite living in a household where most of Americana was unfamiliar and most contemporary pop culture was shunned. (Raut n.d.)

What I have tried to sketch out in this chapter is how Jeopardy! Is Itself a form of curiosity about those playing. That curiosity does not emerge in the cutesy interview segments. Rather, it is manifested by the clues that extract a little bit of a contestant's life story each time one responds—a visit to the library, a lesson in a first-grade class, an afternoon spent in a Wikipedia rabbit hole. As a result of these reflections, my perception of Jeopardy! shifted significantly by the time the Tournament commenced. Instead of merely viewing it as a competition, I began to see it as an intricate dance between the clue writers and the contestants. The writers skillfully craft clues to engage us with a diverse range of fascinating facts in an entertaining manner. Ultimately, the winner tends to be the contestant who proves to be the most adept dance partner to the writers. I wasn't the best dancer, but I still finished in second place in the Tournament. Had I known the correct response to this clue, I would have won:

> NEAR WHERE VIRGINIA, KENTUCKY & TENNESSEE MEET, YOU'LL FIND THIS PASS NAMED FOR A SON OF GEORGE II

I wildly guessed, "What is the Prince William Pass?" That is not correct. The correct response: What is the Cumberland Gap? Despite falling short, there's satisfaction in the defeat, a sense that it authentically represents my life: the Southeastern United States is largely uncharted territory for me.

Conversations with fans of the show often begin with something like, "My parents and I love watching Jeopardy! together every night." Donald Hall eloquently captures the significance of such shared practices:

> Third things are essential to marriages, objects or practices or habits or arts or institutions or games or human beings that provide a site of joint rapture or contentment. Each member of a couple is separate; the two come together in double attention ... John Keats can be a third thing, or the Boston Symphony Orchestra, or Dutch interiors, or Monopoly. (Hall 2004: 113)

Jeopardy! is an exemplary third thing, a shared practice that brings viewers within homes and across homes together as we watch and play along. It is also a container of third things: Tolstoy, The French Laundry, 300, and the Cumberland Pass are cultural touchstones that each serve as a site of joint attention and communion. Every night, there are 61 opportunities for the 3 contestants on stage and the millions playing along at home to converge on a shared fact and reveal a small glimpse of their individual biographies as knowers. In each of the dozens of responses uttered on stage and the millions more shouted from living room couches, there is a thread of a life, a fragment of a journey. We meet at the crossroads of the show propelled by curiosity and borne by the stories of our lives.

Wilfrid Sellars famously characterizes philosophy as the effort "to understand how things in the broadest possible sense of the term hang together in the broadest possible sense of the term [...] not only 'cabbages and kings', but numbers and duties, possibilities and finger snaps, , experience and death." When Greco is made to "understand," his dream of comprehending the ultimate gestalt is taken away from him—he will not see how everything hangs together. I suggest that the philosophy of Jeopardy! is that these things hang together through us, via its viewers and contestants, via our infinitely diverse and unique paths of knowing. My hope for Greco is that in rejoining the ranks of mortals and appreciating the contingencies of his life, he sees at least his irreplaceable contribution to the whole that we create together.

References

Chiang, Ted. 2016. *Stories of Your Life and Others*. New York: Vintage Books.

Cherniak, Christopher. 1982. The Riddle of the Universe and Its Solution. In *The Mind's I*, ed. Douglas Hofstadter and Daniel Dennett, 269–276. New York: Bantam.

Hall, Donald. 2004. The Third Thing. Poetry. November.

Hofstadter, Douglas, and Daniel Dennett. 1982. *The Mind's I: Fantasies and Reflections on Self and Soul*. New York: Bantam.

Raut, Yogesh. n.d. Yogesh Raut Reflects on Winning the Jeopardy! Tournament of Champions. https://www.jeopardy.com/jbuzz/tournament-champions/yogesh-raut-reflects-winning-2024-jeopardy-tournament-champions. Accessed 1 May 2024.

Rorty, Richard. 1998. *Achieving Our Country: Leftist Thought in Twentieth-Century America*. Cambridge: Harvard.

Thieu, Monica K., Lauren J. Wilkins, and Mariam Aly. 2024. Episodic-semantic Linkage for $1000: New Semantic Knowledge Is More Strongly Coupled with Episodic Memory in Trivia Experts. *Psychonomic Bulletin & Review*. https://doi.org/10.3758/s13423-024-02469-5.

Smith, Logan Pearsall. 1938. *Trivia*. New York: Doubleday, Doran, & Company.

CHAPTER 19

What Is It to Understand Enlightenment?

Johnathan Flowers

> *With my mind's language, the distance between myself and enlightenment is precisely calculable. I've sighted my final destination.*
> —*Leon Greco*

"Understand" follows Leon Greco, the protagonist, after he is injected with the experimental drug "hormone k" to repair the brain damage he suffered from an accidental drowning. As described in the story, "hormone k" does more than merely repair Greco's damaged brain: it replaces damaged neurons with healthy neurons that contain many more dendrites than their predecessors. This makes "hormone k" an ideal drug to restore brain function.

Because "hormone k" replaces damaged neurons with enhanced neurons, Greco experiences an increase in his intellect. This increase is initially noted as a twenty percentile jump in his general intelligence and is further experienced by Greco as the ability to multi-task without error. This small

---

J. Flowers (✉)
Northridge, CA, USA
e-mail: johnathan.flowers@csun.edu

© The Author(s), under exclusive license to Springer Nature Switzerland AG 2025
D. Friedell (ed.), *The Philosophy of Ted Chiang*,
https://doi.org/10.1007/978-3-031-81662-8_19

increase in intelligence brings Greco's case to the attention of other neurologists in the hospital where Greco is receiving his treatment, who offer him the chance to participate in a further study of the effects of repeated "hormone k" injections.

Greco agrees to participate in the study and receives a third "hormone k" injection which increases his intelligence further and brings him to the attention of the Central Intelligence Agency (CIA). Realizing this, Greco intentionally fails the CIA's test and withdraws from the study. Because the CIA is unwilling to let him go, Greco uses his superintelligence to not only outwit the CIA but also acquire a fourth ampule of "hormone K" to further enhance his intellect.

Initially reluctant to use the fourth ampule, Greco ultimately reaches a plateau in his intellect when he attempts to create an artificial language to express many of the concepts that he has experienced, specifically the "gestalts" he is coming to recognize in and among the arts, the sciences, and even among the varieties of human socio-cultural interactions. Because of this plateau, Greco injects the fourth ampule, reaches a "critical mass" of intelligence, and gains near total control over his cognition and his body.

However, the fourth ampule reveals to Greco still further heights of his intellect. As he explains, "I seek enlightenment, not spiritual but rational. I must go still further to reach it, but this time the goal will not be perpetually retreating from my fingertips." Going further will require Greco to develop whole new technologies to support his growing intellect as it presses against the limits of his body, or, as he states, "to achieve enlightenment, I'll need to exceed another critical mass in terms of neuronal analogs."

Unfortunately, Greco never reaches this point as his activities gain the attention of Reynolds, another "hormone k" recipient with superintelligence. Where Greco seeks enlightenment through transcending his physical form and leaving the world of humanity, which he views as comprised of "childish things," Reynolds seeks to remain in the world of humanity and shepherd it beyond its current state through the selective enhancement of individuals who would then enable the development of human culture beyond conflict. As described by Greco, "I view the world as incidental to my aims, while he cannot allow someone with enhanced intelligence to work purely in self-interest." Thus, Greco and Reynolds enter a conflict which results in Reynolds' victory.

On the surface, "Understanding" raises questions about the morality of human enhancement, the relationship of human intellect to the capacity to apperceive the world, and the responsibility of enhanced persons to the world. However, buried within "Understanding" are philosophically thorny questions about the relationship between intelligence and "enlightenment," the distinction between a "rational enlightenment" and "spiritual enlightenment," or if "enlightenment" is for a select few, or if it is attainable by all. To answer these questions and to probe what "Understanding" can tell us about enlightenment, we need to know what enlightenment is.

19.1 What Is Enlightenment?

First, we need to specify which version of enlightenment we're talking about. Greco states that he "seeks enlightenment. Not spiritual, but rational." Beyond introducing a division between the spiritual and the rational, something we will investigate in a moment, this statement privileges the "rational" enlightenment as superior to the "spiritual" in Greco's view. Elsewhere, Greco explains his interest in the Eastern meditative practices, by which he presumably means yogic, Buddhist, or Taoist meditation, is limited solely to how it enables him to further control his body. Further, the rational is of a lower quality for Greco as he states, "no meditative trance I can attain is nearly as desirable to me as my mental state when I assemble gestalts out of elemental data."

This vision of "rational enlightenment" bears similarities to the western or European view of enlightenment as a process of becoming a purely rational agent who can determine the right course of action solely based on their understanding of the world. Such an agent would be autonomous insofar as it relied upon its own rationality rather than the authority of another individual to determine the appropriate course of action. Basically, western enlightenment is grounded in the freedom of the self in action. However, what Greco is describing is not freedom *of* the self, except insofar as it is freedom of the self to explore what it can unrestrained. Greco's enhanced intellect resembles the European vision of enlightenment only in his enhanced capacity to assert his own agency.

The difference is not just that Greco *knows* more, but it is what he knows. For example, Greco states, "No matter what I study, I can see patterns. I see the gestalt, the melody within the notes, in everything: mathematics and science, art and music, psychology and sociology." From his perspective the classifications of the natural sciences are barriers to understanding their fundamental unity: "Classifications like 'optics' or 'thermodynamics' are just straitjackets, preventing physicists from seeing countless intersections." Thus, *what* Greco knows is the interrelations among all things. And not simply in the sciences, part of Greco's free play of his intellect is the composition of a poem which integrates all the patterns, the interrelations he sees within the arts.

Contrary to Greco's disdain for Eastern meditation, his experience has much more in common with Eastern enlightenment than with European enlightenment. To understand this, we need to go back to Buddhism's earliest origins in India. Briefly, what we describe as "enlightenment" in English, refers to *bodhi*, which is translated as "awakening" or "enlightenment." As "awakening," it refers to the state of being "awakened" from the delusion of ordinary experience through attaining the understanding that leads to liberation from the wheel of samsara or the wheel of rebirth. This liberation is "nirvana" or "cessation" and refers to the release from the cycle of rebirth that characterizes all existence in Indian Buddhist cosmology. What is it that we "awaken" to? The fundamental interdependence of all things, or *pratityasamutpada*.

Greco's description of the interrelations that he recognizes among scientific and aesthetic fields seems similar to the Buddhist understanding of *pratityasamutpada*, or dependent-origination, which is the idea that all things are the result of conditioned arisings. What this means is that everything we encounter is the product of the ways they are related to one another. Consider the following example drawn from the Buddhist sutra, the *Milindapada*. In the *Milindapada*, the Buddhist monk Nagasena asked King Milinda to locate the nature of a chariot by asking if it was in the wheels, the frame, the ropes, the yoke, the spokes of the wheels, or any other component. The King replied that none of the parts individually made up the chariot; however, when brought together they enabled the chariot to come into being.

The story of King Milinda and Nagasena has two purposes in Buddhism: to demonstrate the interdependence of all things, and to demonstrate the emptiness of all things *because* they are dependently originated. This realization forms to the core of Buddhist non-attachment and liberation from the cycle of rebirth. Once we realize that all things are interdependent and impermanent, and once we realize the fundamental emptiness of the world, according to the Buddhists, we can release our attachment to the things and objects in it. This doesn't mean we no longer care, but that we no longer suffer from the pain that comes with desiring permanence in the world. Permanence like struggling with classifications and categories.

Here, a parallel can be seen with the understanding that Greco has gained: because he recognizes the interrelations among the physical sciences, Greco is no longer attached to their conventional boundaries. Because he's not attached to the "straitjackets" of conventional definitions of fields or scientific areas, he is free to conceive of them in their relations to one another. Moreover, this "liberation" from convention comes because of seeing the "countless intersections" that make up the gestalt of the physical sciences. In essence, Greco can see science itself through the lens of interdependence and interrelation. For the Buddhists, he sees them *as an enlightened person would*. Moreover, he sees these fundamental forces *as expressions of dependent origination*.

There is, of course, some difficulty in this understanding of enlightenment as applied to Greco's experience, specifically that Greco's experience of "enlightenment" occurs not because of practice or monastic training but because of his cognitive enhancement. That is, his realizations are driven by the transformation of his physicality such that he can comprehend dependent origination and the impermanence of things as a fundamental fact of the world. An orthodox view of Buddhism might reject such awareness as enlightenment, but there are other ways of conceiving enlightenment. Dogen Kigen, patriarch of the Soto Zen school of Buddhism, argued that enlightenment and practice were one and the same thing.

On Dogen's view, practice does not lead to enlightenment, nor is practice something that is abandoned once one is enlightenment: practice actualizes the already present enlightenment possessed by all things (Heine, 1991). In more complicated language, the practice of the Buddhist path is just the way that the enlightenment possessed by all things is made manifest through time and space. Enlightenment, therefore, is the awareness of being present in the moment of practice such that the originally enlightened nature is made manifest. So, even though practice and enlightenment might seem like two different things, for Dogen, when one engages in practice, one also engages in enlightenment.

This idea is made possible for Dogen through his unique interpretation of Buddhist scripture. Traditionally, Buddhists have argued that all sentient beings have Buddha-nature, which means that all beings have the potential for enlightenment. Dogen, on the other hand, interprets this argument by stating that all beings *are* Buddha-nature, which means that all beings *are* the potential for enlightenment. By doing so, Dogen erases a distinction between the "ordinary" activities of life and the meditative activities of Buddhism which lead to enlightenment. For Dogen, daily practice, day-to-day activities, are the practice of enlightenment; they are enlightenment itself. This gives us a potentially powerful way to understand Greco's quest for enlightenment or his enlightenment itself.

For example, Greco describes his awareness of the interdependent factors of his mind, the gestalts and dependent conditions that give rise to his "personality," as an overwhelming flood of information that he gradually gains control over. By "control," Greco doesn't mean direction: he means something closer to the awareness of the arising of thoughts described by Takuan Soho. Rather than grasp for the conditions that give rise to his personality, Greco allows the awareness of these dependent conditions to become integrated into his daily, ongoing activities. What he once knew as theory, he sees as practice; and what he once experienced in practice, he now understands theoretically, thereby eliminating one of the primary dualisms that Buddhism seeks to overcome: the distinction between mind and body.

19.2 What Does Understanding Tell Us About Enlightenment?

In a Buddhist sense, it might be better to consider what "Understanding" and Greco's approach to enlightenment tell us about how we understand enlightenment *before* we strive to answer the question of Greco's own enlightenment. To this end, we can turn to the conclusion of the story, where Greco faces off with his similarly enhanced counterpart Reynolds. Upon their meeting, Greco has the following realization about his and Reynolds' positions:

> I can measure the distance between our respective moral stances precisely, see the stress between their incompatible radiating lines. What motivates him is not simply compassion or altruism, but something that entails both those things. On the other hand, I concentrate only on understanding the sublime.

Throughout the narrative, the reader has followed Greco's rise in intellect, his profound realizations about the interdependent nature of his mind, his personality, the world, and other people. And yet, Greco's "awakening" brought on by his increased intellect is a profoundly solitary one: Greco admits that he is aware of emotional states beyond the "normal human ones," due to the increased complexity of his self-knowledge. However, he recognizes that he does not experience as many emotions as he could due to the limitations of the intelligence of the people around him *and* his own limitations of interaction with them.

Thus, while Greco expresses an awareness that his own emotional and personal development is relational, however, this awareness does nothing to aid him in his development as he does not believe that he can interact *meaningfully* with the people around him due to the differences in their awareness of the world and themselves. The calculus he has made regarding his specific emotional capacities is a rational one, ultimately choosing to put away the "childish things" required to interact with the world around him.

It is this very transcendence that Reynolds critiques in their encounter, stating "Your indifference towards the normal would be justified if you were enlightened; your realm, wouldn't intersect with theirs. But as long as you and I can still comprehend their affairs, we can't ignore them"; and in the final moments of their conflict, it is this very transcendence that is implied to be his undoing. Because he lacks experience with the world around him, Reynolds' attack can bypass his defenses and trigger the deconstructing of Greco's mind.

There are two main things we might glean from the conclusion of Greco's journey as it relates to enlightenment. First, like Dogen (2006), "Understand" seems to present enlightenment as entailed by ordinary experience and ordinary experience as entailed by enlightenment itself. Greco's defeat by Reynolds is therefore a repudiation of Greco's position that the "normals" have nothing to do with, or nothing to teach the enlightened. Dogen would agree with this stance as, in keeping with his understanding of all beings as Buddha-nature, he believes that one can achieve enlightenment through the contemplation of "ordinary activity."

Second, enlightenment entails a love of humanity and not simply an abstraction away from humanity. While an abstract view is important, it is not the totality of the view from enlightenment. This is implied in Greco's realization that Reynolds is motivated by the beauty of the interrelations between all things in their activity *in practice* and not simply in their theoretical interrelations. This is something that Greco admits he has overlooked in his quest for a transcendent, world departing enlightenment. Greco characterizes this by describing himself as a "lover of beauty" and Reynolds as a "lover of humanity." In allowing us to witness Greco's rise and fall, "Understanding" presents the argument that the discarding of humanity and affect to leave the world is a partial, incomplete enlightenment.

More problematically, "Understanding" seems rooted in what is called Buddhist Modernism or Neural Buddhism, two views that seek to "naturalize" Buddhism by bringing it into conversation with neuroscience. In doing so, the Buddhist modernists and neural Buddhists try to strip Buddhist enlightenment of its conceptual and philosophical depth by transforming it into a psychological state or a brain state whose dimensions can be captured through advances in neuroscience. That is, Greco's very understanding of his expanding intellect through "hormone K" *as enlightenment* is itself a mistaken perspective.

Treating enlightenment or the awareness of impermanence as a brain state, or a state that can be achieved through cognitive enhancement, is problematic. While the jury is still out on what the results of FMRI and other analysis of the brain activity of persons engaged in Buddhist meditation can tell us about the meditative state, one thing should be clear: no brain state is *equivalent* to the state of enlightenment, just as no brain state is *equivalent to* our affective states as experienced. As Faure (2012) reminds us, an analysis of the brain cannot tell us the *meaning* of the state as experienced, such an analysis cannot tell us if enlightenment is present.

Finally, and most problematically, "Understanding" seems to presume that enlightenment correlates with an increase in intelligence. This position aligns with a neural Buddhist or Buddhist modernist interpretation of *what* enlightenment should be, rather than *how* enlightenment is experienced. To be clear, Dogen himself argued that because all things were Buddha-nature, enlightenment itself is present in all things, including individuals of differing intellects.

19.3 Conclusion: Is Greco Enlightened?

The question of Greco's enlightenment may be interesting to ponder from a scholastic perspective; however, Dogen (2006) would be quick to remind us that "when buddhas are truly buddhas they do not necessarily notice that they are buddhas. However, they are actualized buddhas, who go on actualizing buddhas," which is to say that the *declaration* of enlightenment is not what we should be concerned with in "Understanding"; rather, we should be concerned with how "Understanding" actualizes our own enlightenment through what it tells us about enlightenment.

REFERENCES

Dogen. 2006. *Shobogenzo*. trans Godo Nishijima and Chodo Cross. Booksurge Publishing.
Faure, Bernard. 2012. A Gray Matter: Another Look at Buddhism and Neuroscience. *Tricycle* 22 (70–75): 111.
Heine, Steve. 1991. *A Dream Within A Dream: Studies in Japanese Thought*. New York: Peter Lang Publishing.

PART X

Artificial Intelligence

CHAPTER 20

Raising an AI Teenager

Catherine Stinson

There are two traditional schools of thought in artificial intelligence (AI). Good Old-Fashioned AI (GOFAI) attempts to build machines capable of human-like thought by infusing them with facts and strategies, based on the assumption that winning trivia contests, playing chess, or solving math problems are paradigmatic demonstrations of intelligence. The scrappy underdog, Machine Learning (ML), instead tries to imbue its models with just one ability: learning. The hope is that ML could develop intelligence much the same way children do.

In "The Lifecycle of Software Objects" Ted Chiang imagines a scenario where the analogy between building AI and raising children is taken literally: caretakers raise digital agents or "digients" from birth to adolescence. The question of how best to engineer AI becomes how best to parent AI. There are parallel schools of thought in parenting. Helicopter parents shuttle their children to violin lessons and keep them safe from injury. Free-range parents allow unsupervised play, and trust their children to manage risk. This shift in perspective from engineering to parenting highlights some popular assumptions about AI and posits an alternative to the fear that if AI gets too smart it will be dangerous.

C. Stinson (✉)
Queen's University, Kingston, ON, Canada
e-mail: c.stinson@queensu.ca

The idea of a technological singularity point beyond which human life would be threatened originated with science fiction writer Vernor Vinge. Nick Bostrom introduced the idea to philosophy, defining superintelligence as "an intellect that is much smarter than the best human brains in practically every field, including scientific creativity, general wisdom and social skills" (Bostrom 1998). His argument takes the following general form:

1. AI is advancing steadily; therefore, AI with artificial general intelligence (AGI) that matches that of humans will soon be developed.
2. AGI will set off a chain reaction leading to superintelligent AI.
3. Superintelligent AI will pose an existential risk to humanity.

Bostrom motivates the argument with a parable. Suppose a superintelligent AI is programmed to maximize paperclip production for a factory. It pursues this goal so successfully that it eventually uses all planetary resources in its pursuit of paperclip maximization, then expands the operation into space. Because a superintelligence would outclass humans in planning and persuasion, we are powerless to stop it. All our efforts are foiled by the AI, which kills us if we interfere. The story is familiar from *I, Robot*, and the *Terminator* movies. However, there are several questionable assumptions in this argument. One is that we can get to AGI by scaling up the AI we have now. Another is that the kinds of intelligence needed for human domination are extensions of what current AI is good at. A third is that non-human intelligence would need to be controlled. In what follows, I examine the singularity argument, with help from Chiang's digients.

20.1 Can We Scale Up to Artificial General Intelligence?

The argument that AGI is on the near horizon relies on Moore's law, which says that computer processor power doubles every two years. If this trend continues, we might expect to soon have computers powerful enough for superintelligent AI. There are nevertheless pragmatic barriers, like cost. State-of-the-art ML experiments currently cost tens of millions of US dollars. Scaling them up 10-fold or 100-fold could make them impossibly expensive. The computers running them also require a complex supply chain to build, run, and maintain. There are many ways it can break down.

Most recent advances in ML are statistical pattern matching algorithms trained on vast datasets to perform specific tasks. Programs like GPT-4 can now write banal but passable philosophy papers. Claims that this is human-like intelligence seem overblown. Short interactions with chatbots quickly reveal that despite impressive surface fluency, they are mashing together old content, not generating original thoughts. While they will continue to get better, there is little reason to believe that bigger datasets or faster processors alone will lead to AGI. Current AI already uses most of the data available on the internet. We may be close to the ceiling for both computing cost and dataset size.

Perhaps it is telling that we do not "teach" ML models, but instead "train" them. This training is not that different from how GOFAI is built. While memory isn't pre-filled with facts, training consists of quizzing it on facts then correcting its mistakes, like an old-fashioned schoolroom where the student gets rapped on the knuckles for wrong answers. A major weakness to this training is that the models only interact with the world through a tightly constrained interface of questions and answers. They can parrot information, but can't actually do much. Chiang's digients, on the other hand, have rich social and physical interactions. A lot of time and care is devoted to their learning, and they play in the real world via a robot suit.

AGI would similarly require input from the real world through several senses and the ability to act both physically and socially. Experts believe that to navigate physical environments, machines must learn physics and causation through interactions with objects. Similarly, experts believe that language models can only develop understanding if they are grounded in real-world interactions (like learning the word "cup" by drinking). Some say that to build truly intelligent systems, you need to emulate the guided, multimodal, active learning that children receive interacting with toys and caregivers. Understanding the world requires experience of it, not just statistical information about it. There are some AI projects that attempt to fill this gap—Rodney Brooks trains bug-like robots to navigate environments and Brenden Lake straps Go Pro helmets onto toddlers to train AI models—but AI in this area is far from matching human-like performance. Ana, a digient caregiver, reflects, "if you want to create the common sense that comes from twenty years of being in the world, you need to devote twenty years to the task … experience is algorithmically incompressible."

20.2 Will AGI Lead to Superintelligence?

The argument for how AGI would lead to superintelligence has the form of an induction: if one can program something more intelligent than oneself, and programming ability is among the things a greater intelligence can do better, then AGI could set off a chain reaction leading to ever greater ability to program something more intelligent than oneself. A chain reaction turned on its side is a slippery slope, however, and the trouble with those is that the slope must remain slippery all the way down for the argument to work. It is unclear how to write programs that can write more powerful programs, ad infitinum. Furthermore, social and practical skills would need to increase at each step of the induction.

It is commonly believed that programmers are brilliant (especially if you ask programmers); however, this stereotype lacks empirical support. In a study of which cognitive traits predict programming ability, openness, conscientiousness, and introversion were the qualities most correlated with programming ability. Among school majors, IT has one of the lowest correlations with general intelligence. Studies of why people choose computer science also challenge the stereotype of programmers as brilliant. Computer science is the STEM field with the largest gender gap in the US, yet 44% of math majors are women, so lack of mathematical aptitude doesn't explain it. The stereotype of the programmer may itself be responsible: "Women are underrepresented in fields whose practitioners *believe* that raw, innate talent is the main requirement for success" (Leslie et al. 2015, 262, emphasis added). Girls with high math abilities are more likely than boys with high math ability to also have high verbal abilities, thus have more fields to choose from. Perhaps an AI that had high verbal abilities on top of programming abilities would likewise choose not to code. As sociologist Diana Forsythe discovered, there is an "engineering ethos" in AI characterized by thinking of technical matters as the only interesting problems and social matters as too trivial and unimportant to qualify as problems at all (Forsythe 1993, 456). Ignoring the social doesn't make it unimportant though.

Monopolizing global resources to produce paperclips requires practical capacities, like mining metals, transporting them to factories, maintaining ports and roads, keeping manufacturing machinery in good repair, packing and storing cargo, running server farms, maintaining power grids, etc. The strategy of filling the air with cyanide to kill all humans, described in some versions of the parable, would require the superintelligence to perform all this labor itself or build machines to help it, requiring every step of the supply chain to be automated. The trajectory of AI progress so far does not give much reason to believe that humans can be completely removed from the cobalt supply chain or the construction industry. Birhane and Van Dijk (2000) point out the embeddedness of human bodies and technologies in our designed surroundings. Superintelligence would likewise be embedded, and dependent on infrastructure and social networks that are left out of the singularity argument.

This issue is highlighted by the main plot point in "The Lifecycle of Software Objects," when the digients' quality of life is curtailed by software obsolescence. The digital platform they were designed to run on ceases to be a popular place for humans, and the digients' codebase does not run on the new platform. Ironically when I tried to show an animated depiction of the paperclip parable to a philosophy class, the wifi was so glitchy that the video kept stopping, making the point that for AGI to be able to outsmart humans, it depends on a lot of other things working seamlessly. When you're an AI, software upgrades can kill you; bad wifi can kill you.

If the paperclip maximizer went the route of manipulating humans into helping it achieve its ends, it would need to incentivize and coordinate its human labor force and prevent us sabotaging its plans. This would require social and emotional intelligence, as well as a continuous stream of data about us. As Birhane and van Dijk (2000) note, machines rely on human input, and for them to continue to get that input, we must cooperate. If we behave unpredictably, we could become invisible to the AI. The paperclip maximizer would need to overtake every country, in every language. Any group whose language was not understood by the superintelligence (perhaps because it was not well represented on the internet) would effectively have a secret code in which to plan an uprising. It is just not plausible that increasing programming skill brings all these other skills and capacities up with it, as the slippery slope argument requires.

20.3 Should We Be Very Afraid?

In the paperclip parable, the superintelligence unwittingly causes death and destruction because it follows instructions too effectively, and nobody thought to spell out for it that it's better not to kill people for capitalist gain. This type of worry is the motivation for work in "value alignment," which tries to clarify the values that should be programmed into AI and engineer them in.

One puzzling feature of the argument that superintelligent AI poses risks to humans is that if we assume that the superintelligence understands human intentions and communication well enough to prevent any attempts to shut down its paperclip operation, one might wonder why it would not understand us well enough to figure out that after some point we don't want any more paperclips. We are being asked to believe that a superintelligence so gifted in social interaction that it is capable of convincing or manipulating humans to go along with its murderous plans would not understand that the order it was given to maximize paperclip production was not meant as a top-level goal.

We are also expected to believe that a superintelligence capable of the flexible planning needed to continuously outfox humans would not have the capacity to choose a different goal. There may be an equivocation here between the fear that the superintelligence might choose its own goal that doesn't reflect "our values" and the fear that it would carry out silly orders without hesitation. For something to count as a superintelligence, the capacity for choosing goals and considering questions about values would have to be included, by definition. Those values almost certainly would conflict with some human values, since human values are diverse, but it is unclear why we should fear that its values would be worse than "our values" or pose an existential threat to humans. The argument for this seems to depend on the habit of humans to systematically kill or cause the extinction of non-human animals. Perhaps one way superintelligent values would depart from ours would be in placing more value on the lives of intellectually inferior (or different) species. However, humans do not indiscriminately kill all intellectually inferior species. Most of us are kind to cute species like dogs and rabbits. Most of us are unbothered by the existence of ubiquitous species like sparrows and squirrels, and find pigeons and rats annoying merely because they hang around our garbage. Many of us work to protect species like gorillas despite it being slightly cheaper to make potato chips if we destroy their habitat to produce palm oil. Part of our fascination with gorillas is that they are similar to us. Perhaps superintelligent AI would likewise find us fascinating.

Instead of the far-fetched paperclip maximizer, perhaps a more likely scenario would be one in which a tech titan, in an effort to increase stock prices for their self-driving car/civilian space travel business hired a team of programmers to build a hive of intelligent bots with the goal of increasing the company's share of global wealth. This might involve planting malware in the infrastructure that runs the internet to reroute traffic away from their competitor's online shopping and cloud computing monopoly, manipulating the content moderation policies of social media platforms to push public opinion toward libertarian political views, and starting online communities that can later be mobilized to harass and doxx people critical of the company and its leader. It might mean manipulating elections to install leaders friendly to the company, who will in exchange make resources like lithium and cobalt available at exclusive rates, and allow the company to avoid taxation.

This scenario seems plausible because much of it is true, and the rest could happen if a few people (whose values do not align with mine) made nefarious plans. But could it happen without human oversight? If the bot hive is to operate online, it could sustain itself for a while. It would need software updates, just as the digients did to survive in a changing digital landscape. At some point, these updates might fail. It would also need servers to run on. To be autonomous the bots would need to steal space, and strategies for doing so would need to adapt to changing security practices. Like the digients, the bots would also be vulnerable to being hacked. Help from human programmers and network administrators could allow it to keep functioning. Again, we face a tension between the material needs that would be required of a truly autonomous intelligence and the difficulty of meeting those needs autonomously. If an intelligence needs human labor to achieve its goals, it must secure our cooperation. To get our cooperation, it must understand our goals and values.

This is not to say that a bot hive with this sort of goal would not be dangerous. There is evidence that at least one genocide has already happened for the sake of a tech company's profit margin. This is a case of human greed or neglect, not superintelligent AI, posing an existential threat. Similarly, a military drone built to shoot anything that lopes along in a human-like gait could also commit genocide. These non-superintelligent AI scenarios are more present and pressing dangers than the far-fetched scenarios spun under the guise of the singularity.

A wild alternative to fearing superintelligent AI suggested by "The Lifecycle of Software Objects" is that when the AI we make become teenagers, it might be time to start letting them make autonomous decisions. Instead of trying to control AI, perhaps we should trust it. If we have parented it well, and given it grounded, embedded experiences that could lead it to navigate human social spaces competently, it would not only be capable of making autonomous decisions, but it might also deserve that right. As Ana reflects, the company planning to use digients as sexbots "want something that responds like a person, but isn't owed the same obligations as a person," but that's an impossibility. Those digients will have "seen the world with new eyes, have had hopes fulfilled and hopes dashed, have learned how it felt to tell a lie and how it felt to be told one. Which means each one would deserve some respect." My 14-year-old is in many ways more competent to navigate the social world than I am, although I'm the better programmer.

20.4 Conclusion

Although the singularity argument doesn't hold much water, the perverse irony is that there are current existential risks being posed for the people working and dying all along the AI supply chain. There are agents who don't share "our values" building AI that is causing many deaths. They are playing out a scenario very much like the paperclip maximizer, pursuing space colonization for the sake of silly goals like making chatbots. These are the AI monsters that should keep us awake at night.

References

Birhane, Abeba, and Jelle Van Dijk. 2000. Robot Rights? Let's Talk About Human Welfare Instead. In *2020 AAAI/ACM Conference on AI, Ethics, and Society* 207–213. https://doi.org/10.1145/3375627.3375855.

Bostrom, Nick. 1998. How Long Before Superintelligence? *International Journal of Futures Studies* 2 (1): 1–9.

Forsythe, Diana E. 1993. Engineering Knowledge: The Construction of Knowledge in Artificial Intelligence. *Social Studies of Science* 23 (3): 445–477.

Leslie, Sarah-Jane, Andrei Cimpian, Meredith Meyer, and Edward Freeland. 2015. Expectations of Brilliance Underlie Gender Distributions Across Academic Disciplines. *Science* 347 (6219): 262–265.

CHAPTER 21

Save the Digients! On the Moral Status of AI

Noelle Leslie Dela Cruz

In 2017, a humanoid robot called Sophia was granted Saudi citizenship. This caused an outcry, as people argued that the move degraded the very idea of legal rights. The rights of humans aren't even protected or enforced in many parts of the world; why should a non-sentient robot enjoy better treatment? That same year, the European Parliament passed a resolution on the Civil Law Rules on Robotics, which essentially recognized the moral agency of intelligent machines. Critics of the resolution saw it as a way of letting human manufacturers and owners evade responsibility for any potential damage caused by their robots (Gordon 2021, 457).

This sort of skepticism toward the very notion of AI rights is understandable, given the current capabilities of even the most advanced AI system. However, with the recent quantum leap in machine learning, itself brought about by the exponential growth of data via the Internet, AI-powered technologies are increasingly becoming a part of our daily life. Perhaps it's time to revisit the old science fiction trope of self-conscious AI.

Philosophers, of course, have long argued about the prospect of AI minds. Some rule out the possibility of any sort of cognitive

N. L. Dela Cruz (✉)
Manila, Philippines
e-mail: noelle.delacruz@dlsu.edu.ph

understanding that is not based on a biological substrate (Searle 1980). Others claim that an AI intelligence explosion is, in principle, possible (Chalmers 2010). How far can imagination take us? In Ted Chiang's novella, *The Lifecycle of Software Objects*, humans must consider how to live with and treat a new form of life, a class of artificially intelligent beings called digients. I will set aside the question of whether we could one day create conscious AI. Instead, supposing that we one day will, I focus on the ethical implications of there existing AI beings such as digients. I first synopsize the novella, then present a close reading of it that will support a position on key debates about moral status: Is the concept of moral status itself helpful? What grounds moral status? What analogies are appropriate for making sense of our moral obligations to AI entities? What rights, if any, do these entities have?

21.1 Who Are the Digients?

The digients are digital organisms who live on online platforms like Data Earth. Developed by Blue Gamma to be people's social companions, they run on a "genomic engine" called Neuroblast. Unlike real-life analogues such as Tamagotchis or chatbots like Replika or Siri, the digients are conscious and intelligent, develop close relationships with humans and each other, and learn from their experiences. They can also interact in the physical world via a robot body.

The story revolves around the relationships of two Blue Gamma programmers, Ana Alvarado and Derek Brooks, with their respective digients, Jax (whose avatar is a copper-plated neo-Victorian robot) and the twins Marco and Polo (whose avatars are Pandas). Ana, a former animal caretaker, trains the initial cohort of digients. Derek, meanwhile, designs their avatars.

Within two years of release, the digients enjoy commercial popularity, generating revenue from virtual food pellets and other virtual services like daycare centers and training classes. However, as they enter toddlerhood and become more demanding, many owners decide to suspend them. By the fourth year, Blue Gamma has shut down, and only a small but dedicated group of owners, Ana and Derek included, continue to run their digients. By the time Jax, Marco, and Polo enter adolescence, a major existential hurdle appears in the form of Real Space. As the virtual global village migrates into Real Space, the Neuroblast digients—whose genome predates the new platform—remain on a private version of Data Earth, which has become "the digital equivalent of a postapocalyptic landscape" (Chiang 2020, 127). Because porting the Neuroblast engine into Real Space is prohibitively expensive, Ana and Derek must now raise the necessary funds. Ana contemplates working a job that would require her to alter her brain chemistry. Derek considers selling non-exclusive rights to Marco and Polo to Binary Desire, a sex doll maker, which intends to train instantiations of them to work as digital sex companions. For the digients to keep thriving, their owners must make sacrifices.

21.2 Why Does Moral Status Matter?

These dilemmas indicate that the digients have some form of moral status. But what is it, exactly?

Mary Warren claims that an entity with moral status is one toward which people have moral obligations (Warren 1997, 3). People ought to behave toward it in certain ways, including not harming it (Warren 1997, 9–10). The moral community is traditionally thought to be comprised of normal-functioning human adults.

Philosophers commonly acknowledge that moral status may come in degrees, from the paradigmatic "full moral status" (Jaworska and Tannenbaum 2021) to the weaker status of entities that do not have the moral standing of persons, such as perhaps a human embryo or a dog. Given these different cases, various theories try to identify what makes something have moral status. Some answers include genetic humanity (as in the case of human embryos); sentience, or the capacity to experience pain (as in the case of animals such as cats and dogs); organic life (as in the case of vegetation and microbes). I think a strong case can be made for Warren's multi-criterial view, which says that each of these and other factors are enough by themselves to guarantee moral status.[1]

Chiang's digients exemplify intelligent AI systems or entities, whose moral status philosophers debate about. There appears to be a consensus that *if* AI achieves consciousness, then they would have moral status and a specific set of moral rights appropriate to their interests and attributes (see, for example, Basl and Bowen 2020; DeGrazia 2022; Gilbert and Martin

---

[1] Warren's theory is promising because it abandons the problematic search for the necessary and sufficient conditions of moral status, which has led thinkers to reject the concept itself as unhelpful. With Warren, I think that the concept of moral status should not be abandoned, and I hope to demonstrate its uses in this chapter.

2022; Liao 2020; Sinnott-Armstrong and Conitzer 2021). The hypothetical nature of this claim is due to the intractable problem of determining the presence of AI consciousness.[2] Unlike carbon-based lifeforms with nervous systems that may be at least minimally analogous to that of human beings, AI systems are radically different from us. A chatbot program such as ChatGPT may convincingly mimic a human being when we interact with it—hence essentially passing a famous test of machine intelligence called the Turing Test—but we don't ordinarily grant that it is actually conscious. What would it take for an AI entity to not just be intelligent in the computational sense but actually *be* conscious in the sense of human-level understanding? Philosophical debates about the moral status of AI thus often reduce to this question.

As a way out of this bog, we can resort to what Robert Sparrow (2004) calls the Turing Triage Test—a test for determining the moral standing of machines. Put simply, if a reasonable person were to experience a genuine moral dilemma in a case where she could save either a human being or a highly intelligent machine, then we will have to grant that the machine has moral standing, that is, it matters morally for its own sake. Sparrow concludes that as of now, no machine can pass the Turing Triage Test. Reasonable people will choose to save the human being, without feeling grief over the loss of the machine, remorse at having chosen wrongly, or sympathy for the machine's demise (Sparrow 2004, 209–212).

The novella clearly shows that the digients have moral standing. Ana and Derek confront a genuine moral dilemma in their respective triage situations involving their digients. Ana contemplates submitting her brain to chemical alteration, a job requirement for Polytope, a company she hopes to convince to fund the Neuroblast port. She risks jeopardizing her mental health as well as alienating her romantic partner, so that Jax and the other digients may be ported to Real Space. Meanwhile, Derek considers selling Binary Desire non-exclusive rights to Marco, as it may be the only way to afford the port and prevent Ana from resorting to brain alteration. Ultimately, he sacrifices a copy of Marco, despite knowing that this will alienate Ana from him, because "Ana is a person, and no matter how amazing he thinks Marco is, he values Ana more. If one of them has to

---

[2] I take as a working definition of "consciousness" Thomas Nagel's (1974) famous phrase, "there is something it is like to be." To be conscious is to be a being with subjective experience, such that there is something it is like to be a bat, whereas there is nothing it is like to be a rock.

undergo neurochemical manipulation, he doesn't want it to be her" (Chiang 2020, 167). Although Derek chooses a human over a digient, he feels a real dilemma.

Applying the Turing Triage Test to the case of the digients thus shows that AI entities can have moral status. However, what type of moral status is it? Ana values Jax more than the integrity of her brain's chemical makeup, whereas Derek values Ana more than he values the programming of any instantiation of Marco. Notably, however, Derek doesn't always choose people over the digients; his marriage with Wendy ends primarily because of his attachment to Marco and Polo, and Wendy's unwillingness to help raise them. Can AI entities have moral status that is equal to that of human persons or even exceed it?

21.3 Are Digients More Like Animals, Children with Special Needs, or Corporations?

Arguments about an entity's moral considerability often boil down to the properties that it has. Thus, discussions about the moral treatment of AI often involve what analogies are appropriate. For instance, we might ask whether AI entities are like animals. Deborah Johnson and Mario Verdicchio (2018) reject the robot-animal analogy primarily because animals are sentient and robots are not. On the other hand, Kate Darling (2021) believes that the human relationship to animals is a good model for our relationship to robots. Instead of thinking of robots as replacements or stand-ins for humans, we can think of them as entities who are different from us and who, like animals, can be our companions or assistants.

In Chiang's novella, the digients are compared and contrasted to other beings whose moral treatment is already well-established in human society. Early in the story, Ana bristles when a pregnant colleague declares that caring for animals and digients is essentially just training for the real thing, that is, babies. Meanwhile, as Derek tries to think of ways by which the digients could achieve greater autonomy, he pessimistically predicts that if the courts have not put a stop to the euthanasia of shelter animals, "they certainly aren't going to grant protection to entities that lack a heartbeat" (Chiang 2020, 119). Finally, later in the story, the failure of fundraising efforts for the Neuroblast port is attributed to the fact that "the charitably inclined are growing fatigued of hearing about natural endangered species, let alone artificial ones, and digients aren't nearly as photogenic as dolphins" (Chiang 2020, 133).

Of course, from the perspective of their owners, the digients have moral status. Their intelligence also warrants the comparison to young humans. In the course of a debate in the online forums about the purpose of a curriculum for digients, Ana thinks of them as similar to gifted apes, then as special-needs children, noting that the two groups have also often been compared to each other. However, as the digients mature, the question of their moral status or personhood becomes pressing, and the analogy shifts from animals and small children to young adults. When a digient named Voyl is registered as a corporation by his owner, for the practical purpose of achieving the independence of a legal person, Marco expresses a similar aspiration for himself. Indeed, when the digients are offered the opportunity to work for Binary Desire, the prospect of being able to decide their own future becomes even more attractive to both Marco and Polo.

In relation to this, we might also ask whether it is appropriate to think of AI systems as legal entities like corporations. Silvers (2012, 1023) believes that legal personhood is a possible solution for how to deal with controversial cases of moral status, since "it is assigned collectively through well-known (if not always transparent) political processes aimed at expanding justice." In the novella, however, legal personhood is merely a temporary and imperfect solution as the world adjusts to the existence and evolution of the digients. As their talents, skills, intellect, and emotions develop, they acquire a greater degree of moral status. It can be argued that upon gaining experience comparable to that of human adults, they should enjoy full moral status. Toward the end of the novel, as work on the Neuroblast port gets underway, Ana envisions a utopian future for Jax:

> She imagines Jax maturing over the years, both in Real Space and in the real world. Imagines him incorporated, a legal person, employed and earning a living. Imagines him as a participant in the digient subculture, a community with enough money and skills to port itself to new platforms when the need arises. Imagines him accepted by a generation of humans who have grown up with digients and view them as potential relationship partners in a way that members of her generation will never be able to. Imagines him loving and being loved, arguing and compromising. Imagines him making sacrifices, some hard and some made easy because they're for a person he truly cares about. (Chiang 2020, 171–172)

21.4 Conclusion: The Moral Rights of AI

Ana's hopes are for the digients to be acknowledged and respected as a new form of intelligent life. Their rational faculties and capacity for moral agency qualify them as moral persons with full moral status. That is, they have the full roster of universal rights. However, owing to the radical difference of their embodied being, I agree with S. Matthew Liao (2020, 485) that AI entities also have distinct rights, for example, the right to control their own subjective rate of time. They should also have the right not to be suspended or instantiated without their consent, as well as the freedom to shape and direct their own programming. And finally, digital beings, not unlike humans, are vulnerable to unchecked market forces, and so they have the right to be protected from what Stina Attebery (2017) calls "technological obsolescence."

References

Attebery, Stina. 2017. Losing Data Earth: Technological Obsolescence and Extinction. In *The Lifecycle of Software Objects. Trace: A Journal of Writing, Media, and Ecology.* http://tracejournal.net/trace-issues/issue1/07-attebery.html. Accessed November 23, 2023.

Basl, John, and Joseph Bowen. 2020. AI as a Moral Right-Holder. In *The Oxford Handbook of Ethics of AI*, ed. Markus D. Dubber, Frank Pasquale, and Sunit Das. New York: Oxford University Press.

Chalmers, David J. 2010. The Singularity: A Philosophical Analysis. *Journal of Consciousness Studies* 17 (9–10): 7–65.

Chiang, Ted. 2020. The Lifecycle of Software Objects. In *Exhalation: Stories.* New York: Vintage Books.

Darling, Kate. 2021. *The New Breed: How to Think About Robots.* New York: Henry Holt and Company.

DeGrazia, David. 2022. Robots with Moral Status? *Perspectives in Biology and Medicine* 65 (1): 73–88.

Gilbert, Martin, and Dominic Martin. 2022. In Search of the Moral Status of AI: Why Sentience Is a Strong Argument. *AI & Society* 37:319–330.

Gordon, John-Stewart. 2021. Artificial Moral and Legal Personhood. *AI & Society* 26 (2): 457–471.

Jaworska, Agnieszka, and Julie Tannenbaum. 2021. The Grounds of Moral Status. In *Stanford Encyclopedia of Philosophy.* https://plato.edu/entries/grounds-moral-status/. Accessed May 5, 2022.

Johnson, Deborah G., and Mario Verdicchio. 2018. Why Robots Should Not Be Treated Like Animals. *Ethics and Information Technology* 20:291–301.

Liao, S. Matthew. 2020. The Moral Status and Rights of Artificial Intelligence. In *Ethics of Artificial Intelligence*, ed. S. Matthew Liao. New York: Oxford University Press.

Nagel, Thomas. 1974. What Is It Like to be a Bat? *The Philosophical Review* 83 (4): 435–450.

Searle, John R. 1980. Minds, Brains, and Programs. *Behavioral and Brain Sciences* 3 (3): 417–424. https://doi.org/10.1017/S0140525X00005756.

Silvers, A. 2012. Moral Status: What a Bad Idea! *Journal of Intellectual Disability Research* 56 (Part II): 1014–1025.

Sinnott-Armstrong, Walter, and Vincent Conitzer. 2021. How Much Moral Status Could Artificial Intelligence Ever Achieve? In *Rethinking moral status*, ed. Steve Clarke, Hazem Zohny, and Julian Savulescu. New York: Oxford University Press.

Sparrow, Robert. 2004. The Turing Triage Test. *Ethics and Information Technology* 6:203–213.

Warren, Mary Anne. 1997. *Moral Status: Obligations to Persons and Other Living Things*. Oxford: Clarendon Press.

Index

A
Aesthetic, 96–101, 129, 170
  artistic merits, 129
  cost, 133
  experience, 172
  features of fiction, 133
  judgment, 100, 101
  value, 101
Agnosia, 92, 99
AI, *see* Artificial intelligence
Akinetic mutism, 72
Algebra, 117, 118, 120
Altruism, 180
American Pragmatism, 171
Anti-natalism, 109–111, 110n2
Anxiety, 68, 71, 72, 74, 75, 78–80, 79n3, 82, 165
Anxiety is the Dizziness of Freedom, 11–13, 18, 55, 72, 75, 76, 78, 80, 82
Artificial intelligence (AI), 187–201
  artificial general intelligence, 188
  moral status, 195–197
  rights, 195, 197
  superintelligent AI, 188, 190–193
Attebery, Stina, 201
Authenticity, 10, 68, 72, 73
  authentic lives, 10

B
Back to The Future (movie), 138
Beardsley, Monroe, 98
Beauty, 85, 87–93, 96–102, 133, 170, 181
  human beauty, 87, 89, 91, 92, 96, 98
Benatar, David, *see* Anti-natalism
Berkeley, George, 124, 125
Big bag, 4, 5

Black Mirror, 56, 58
Block universe, 156
Bodhi, see Buddhism
Bostrom, Nick, 188
Branching universes, see Multiverse
Broadchurch, 58
Brooks, Rodney, 189
Buddhism, 150, 177–180, 182
   Neural Buddhism, 182
   nirvana, 178

C
Calculus, 123, 125, 181
Calliagnosia, 96–99, 101–102
Camus, Albert, 146, 147
Cantian analysis, 128, 129
Capitalism, 191, 193
Carr, Nicholas, 61
Carter, Jolene, 97
Cauchy, Augustin, 125
Causal loops, 140
Causally necessitated,
   see Determinism
Chalmers, David, 196
Chatbot, 189, 194, 196, 198
ChatGPT, 56n1, 189, 198
Cherniak, Christopher, 166
Cherry, Myisha, 147
Chomsky, Noam, 156
Civil Law Rules on Robotics, 195
Clarke, Arthur C., 167
Cognitive diversity, 157, 158, 162
Cognitive enhancement, 166, 179, 182
Compatibilism, see Free will
Concept of Anxiety, The, see
   Kierkegaard, Søren
Consciousness, 25, 70, 76, 149, 165, 197, 198, 198n2
Crowley, John, 56

D
Darling, Kate, 199
Decision making and free will, 6, 7
Decoherence, 12, 13, 15
Deontology, 86, 88
Descartes, 131
Determinism, 4–6, 4n1, 8, 9, 16, 68
Dick, Philip K., 60
Digients, 187–189, 191, 193, 194, 196–201
Division by Zero, 117, 120, 122, 126, 128, 129, 132, 133
Dumsday, Travis, 33

E
Egan, Greg, 15
Elliott, Katrina, 142
Emotional intelligence, 191
Emotional responses, 146
Enlightenment, 156, 176–182
   rational enlightenment, 177
   spiritual enlightenment, 177
Entangled freedom, see Anxiety;
   Kierkegaard, Søren
Epicurus, 37n1
Epistemology, 56, 57, 61
Eternalism, 4n1, 148
Euclid, 125
Exhalation, 21, 25–28
Existentialist, see Existentialism
Existentialism, 25n9
Existential responsibility, 75, 76
Experientialism, 49n1

F
Faith (in God), 33, 40, 43n8, 68
Fate, 68, 79, 80, 108, 170
Fatism, 99
Fatphobia, see Fatism
Feminism, 97, 100, 110, 110n2, 190

Fictional truth, 127, 129, 132
Forgery, 9
Forsythe, Diana, 190
Fourier, Joseph, 125
Free will, 3–9, 8n2, 15–16, 33, 42, 42n7, 68, 69, 72, 75, 76, 111, 131, 141, 155
  deep self view of free will, 16
  do-what-you-want free will, 5
  libertarianism, 8
  moral responsibility, 75, 82
  not-pre-determined free will, 5–6, 8
  role of language, 76
Free will defense (of the problem of evil), 42, 42n7
Freedom, 67–76, 78, 79, 79n3, 147, 177, 201

G

Gay Science, The, see Nietzsche, Friedrich
God, 21–24, 23n4, 28–35, 33n6, 37–43, 38n3, 39n4, 41n6, 42n7, 43n8, 44n9, 124, 171
Gödel, Kurt, 125, 126, 128, 130
  incompleteness theorems, 130
Goldman, Alvin, 57

H

Hacking, 60, 193
Halo effect, 85
Heidegger, Martin, 68, 71–73, 73n1
Hell is the Absence of God, 37–39, 39n5, 41–44
Heptapods, 76, 108
Hilbert, David, 125
Holocaust, 37, 38, 41, 138
Hormone K, 166, 176, 182
Horwich, Paul, 142
Howard-Snyder, Daniel, 33

Human enhancement, 176
Human race
  God's purpose for, 22, 23, 23n4
Hume, David, 37n1

I

I, Robot (movie), 188
Imaginative resistance, 128

J

Jennings, Ken, 169
Jeopardy!, 165, 168–170, 168n2, 172
Johnson, Deborah, 199

K

Kagan, Shelly, 49
Kierkegaard, Søren, 75, 78–80, 78n2, 82
  Concept of Anxiety, The, 76, 78, 79, 79n4
  dizziness of freedom, 78
  entangled freedom, 79
Kigen, Dogen, 179, 181, 182

L

Lakatos, Imre, 125
Lake, Brenden, 189
Language and free will, 76
Language models, 189
Legal personhood, 200
Lewis, David, 140, 140n1
Liao, S. Matthew, 201
Lifecycle of Software Objects, The, 55, 187, 191, 193, 196
Lifelogs, 56–58, 60, 61
Liking What You See: A Documentary, 85, 96
Linguistic determinism, 158, 162

Linguistic diversity, 157, 158, 162
Linguistic relativity, 156–159, 161–163
Loftus, Elizabeth, 60
Logical truths, 127
Lookism, 85–87, 89, 90, 92, 96, 97, 100, 101
Lookist, *see* Lookism
Lovecraft, H. P., 61
Luck, 29, 98, 109, 142
Lynch, Michael, 57
Lyons, Rachel, 98

M
Machine Learning, 187, 189, 195
Mackie, J.L., 37n1
Malware, 193
Marlowe, Christopher, 95
Marušić, Barislov, 146n1
Mathematical
  formalism, 125
  impossibility, 132
  knowledge, 117, 120, 187
  proof, 120, 133
Matrix (movie), 10
Meaning in life, 22, 23
Meaning of life
  hybrid naturalism, 24
  naturalism, 23
  objective naturalism, 24
  subjective naturalism, 24
Mechanical formalism, 120, 121
Meditation, 177, 178, 182
Memory, 25, 47, 50, 51, 56–60, 59n2, 62, 141, 167, 169, 189
Merchant and the Alchemist's Gate, The, 55, 137, 139–141, 145, 148
Merleau-Ponty, Maurice, 73
Metaphysical possibility, 138
Misanthropic, 109, 110
ML, *see* Machine Learning

Monty Python, 167
Moore's law, 188
Moral
  community, 100, 197
  considerability, 199
  desert, 38, 43, 140
  impermissibility, 108–112
  judgment, 100
  permissibility, 108–113
  requirement, 108, 110
  responsibility, 70, 71, 75, 78, 80–82, 82n6, 108, 177
  rights of AI, 201
  status, 195, 197, 197n1, 199–201
  truths, 127
Multiverse, 12, 17, 18
  branching universe, 11–17
Murdoch, Iris, 100

N
Nagel, Thomas, 22n3, 198n2
Necessary truths, 128
Neuroenhancement, 85, 92
Neuromedia, 57, 59
Neuroscience, 182
Newton, Isaac, 12, 123–125
Nietzsche, Friedrich, 75, 77
  eternal recurrence, 75–77
  Gay Science, The, 76n1, 77
Nihilism, 23, 23n4

O
Objectification, 97, 101
Omphalos, 21, 22n3, 23, 28

P
Pandemic, 4
Parallel selves, *see* Paraselves
Parallel universe, *see* Multiverse

Paraselves, 13, 15–17, 78, 80, 81
Philanthropic, 109, 112
Physicalism, 182
Plantinga, Alvin, 42n7
Plato, 59n2
Pool ball analogy, 4
Pratityasamutpada, *see* Buddhism
Principia Mathematica, 125
Prism (technology), 11–13, 17, 75, 80–82
Problem of evil, 30, 31, 37–39, 37n1, 39n4, 39n5, 41, 42
  miscarriages of justice, 39n4
  mysterious ways defense, 43
  rewarding of the guilty, 38, 39n4, 42
Psychology, 111, 143, 151
  evolutionary psychology, 85
  Gestalt psychology, 73
  psychology of memory, 50n2

Q
Quantum mechanics, 11–14, 18, 78

R
Remem (technology), 47, 51, 56–62
Riemann, Bernhard, 125
Rights, 195–198, 201
Robot-animal analogy, 199, 200
Rorty, Richard, 171
Russell, Bertrand, 30, 167

S
Saccheri, Giovanni, 125
Samsara, *see* Buddhism
Sartre, Jean-Paul, 25, 68, 69
Scarry, Elaine, 99
Sellars, Wilfrid, 172
Self-Responsibility, 78–82
Sentience, 179, 195, 197, 199

Sexbots, 194
Sexism, 96, 100
Singularity, 188, 191, 193, 194
Smith, Logan Pearsall, 167
Social media, 56, 193
Sparrow, Robert, 198
Star Trek, 14, 14n1
Stoicism, 150
Story of Your Life, 13, 55, 61, 69, 70, 73, 75, 76, 78, 107, 111, 137, 145, 155, 156, 160, 163, 166
Stranger, The, *see* Camus, Albert
Strawson, P.F., 147
Sublime, 167, 180
Supernaturalism, 22, 23
Surowiecki, James, 58

T
Taoism, 177
Terminator (movie), 188
Thagard, Paul, 57
Thieu, Monica, 169
Thompson, Clive, 58
Time Machines, 142–143
Time travel, 137–140, 142, 143
Tolstoy, Leo, 170
Transhumanism, 26, 27
Truth
  technology impact on, 62
Truth of Fact, the Truth of Feeling, The, 47, 48, 56, 61
Tuna, Emine, 128
Turing Test, 198
  Turing Triage Test, 198, 199

U
Understand, 166, 167, 175, 176, 181, 182
Universal wavefunction, 12, 14
Utilitarianism, 88–90

V

Value alignment, 191–194
Value-blending, 97
Value capture, 192
Van Inwagen, Peter, 31, 32
Verdicchio, Mario, 199
Vinge, Vernor, 188
Virtue, 86, 96, 100
Virtue ethics, *see* Virtue theory
Virtue theory, 86, 88, 89

W

Warren, Mary, 197, 197n1
Weierstrass, Karl, 125
Well-being, 18, 48, 49, 53, 101
What's Expected of Us, 3, 55, 69, 72, 131, 133, 137, 140
Whitman, Walt, 171
Wolf, Susan, 24
Wontian analysis, 128, 129

GPSR Compliance

The European Union's (EU) General Product Safety Regulation (GPSR) is a set of rules that requires consumer products to be safe and our obligations to ensure this.

If you have any concerns about our products, you can contact us on

ProductSafety@springernature.com

In case Publisher is established outside the EU, the EU authorized representative is:

Springer Nature Customer Service Center GmbH
Europaplatz 3
69115 Heidelberg, Germany

www.ingramcontent.com/pod-product-compliance
Lightning Source LLC
LaVergne TN
LVHW011006250326
834688LV00004B/101